Einführung von Grammatik
im Englischunterricht

Einführung von Grammatik im Englischunterricht

Materialien und Modelle
von Detlef und
Margaret von Ziegésar

Ehrenwirth

Die Deutsche Bibliothek – CIP-Einheitsaufnahme

Ziegésar, Detlef von:
Einführung von Grammatik im Englischunterricht :
Materialien und Modelle / von Detlef und Margaret von
Ziegésar. – München : Ehrenwirth, 1992
   ISBN 3-431-03166-8
NE: Ziegésar, Margaret von:

ISBN 3-431-03166-8

© 1992 by Ehrenwirth Verlag GmbH,
Schwanthalerstraße 91, 8000 München 2
Zeichnungen: Eduard Wienerl
Satz: Fotosatz-Service Weihrauch, Würzburg
Druck: Druckerei Mühlberger, Gersthofen
Printed in Germany 1992

Inhalt

Vorwort

Vorwort

Erwerbsorientierter Grammatikunterricht

Dieses praxisorientierte Buch bedient sich einer aus langjähriger Erprobung erwachsenen und sprachlernpsychologisch begründeten Methode, mit der die wichtigsten grammatischen Strukturen der englischen Sprache kommunikativ eingeführt und die ersten grundlegenden Übungen vorgenommen werden können. Es gibt den Lehrern und Lehrerinnen für die von den Lehrwerken oft vernachlässigte Einführungsphase eine zusätzliche Hilfe, wie sie diese Phase für die Lernenden motivierender, transparenter, weniger angstbesetzt und sprachlich ergiebiger gestalten können.

Obwohl die dem Buche zugrundeliegende *erwerbsorientierte* Methode speziell zur Grammatikeinführung konzipiert wurde, läßt sie sich ebenso wirkungsvoll zur Grammatikwiederholung einsetzen.

Für jede der 46 Strukturen liegt ein methodisch und sprachlich detailliert ausgearbeitetes Unterrichtsmodell vor, das entweder direkt für den Unterricht übernommen oder aber den individuellen Bedürfnissen der Lernenden angepaßt werden kann.

Die Modelle sind so flexibel, daß sie je nach Bedarf in 30–45 Minuten durchgenommen werden können.

Auswahl, Progression und inhaltliche Gestaltung der Strukturen ermöglichen die Verwendung des Buches sowohl in Haupt- und Realschulen als auch in Gymnasien und im Erwachsenenbereich.

Alle Strukturen sind einerseits in natürliche Kommunikationssituationen eingebettet, andererseits wird die von den Lehrplänen der verschiedenen Bundesländer vorgeschriebene und in Lehrwerken verwirklichte Strukturenprogression eingehalten. Dadurch stellt dieses Buch eine optimale Ergänzung eines jeden Lehrwerkes dar, die gesammelten Unterrichtsmodelle sind dem Vokabel-, Strukturen- und Weltwissen der Lernenden angepaßt, die Strukturen werden kommunikativ verwendet, und das formal-grammatische Üben ist gewährleistet.

Die Methode geht in fünf, die natürlichen Spracherwerbsprinzipien nützenden Schritten vor:

I Demonstration

Die Struktur wird in einem Lehrer-Demonstrationsgespräch vorgeführt. Die Situationen in den Unterrichtsmodellen wurden so gewählt, daß sie für die Lernenden lebendig, interessant und klar sind, daß die Strukturen situationsangemessen verwendet werden und daß sie der Lehrende je nach Bedarf bis zu 15mal zwanglos vorsprechen kann.

II Verstehen und Reagieren

In diesem Schritt beweisen die Lernenden, daß sie die neue Struktur hörend verstehen. Sie reagieren sprachlich darauf, indem sie die neue Struktur jedoch selbst noch nicht verwenden, sondern mit ihnen schon bekannten Sprachmitteln antworten. Dadurch haben sie genügend Zeit, das neue Sprachmaterial in Ruhe zu verarbeiten, und werden durch eine verfrühte, erzwungene Verwendung nicht verunsichert.

III Reproduzieren

Erst in diesem Schritt verwenden die Lernenden die neue Struktur selbst. Im Dialog mit dem Lehrer wird ihnen die Struktur kommunikativ sinnvoll jedoch immer wieder zugespielt, so daß diese außer situationsbedingten, geringfügigen Veränderungen von Vokabeln lediglich reproduziert werden muß.

IV Produzieren

Hauptsächlich in Gruppen- und Partnerarbeit verwenden die Lernenden die Struktur erstmals selbständig. Die Aufgaben sind so gewählt, daß die Lernenden gemäß den Zielen des kommunikativen und interaktiven Fremdsprachenunterrichts erfahren, mit dem neuen Sprachmittel konkret etwas erreichen zu können.

V Bewußtmachung

Eine bewußte Formulierung der Grammatikregel erfolgt in den meisten Fällen erst im V. Schritt, nachdem die Lernenden eine ausreichend große Spracherfahrung gemacht und sowohl den pragmatisch-semantischen Gehalt als auch die formal-grammatische Struktur des neuen Sprachmittels schon einigermaßen durchschaut haben. Die Regeln werden von den Schülern unter Mithilfe des Lehrers soweit wie nötig induktiv erarbeitet. Eine adressatengemäße Regelformulierung wird am Ende jedes Unterrichtsmodells gegeben.

Die in den Unterrichtsmodellen verwendeten Materialien sind Tageslichtprojektor-Folien, Arbeitsblätter und Satzkarten. Einfache Strichzeichnungen, Tabellen etc. lassen sich leicht kopieren. Sind die wenig zeitaufwendigen Materialien einmal erstellt, bilden sie eine bleibende Grundlage für den in diesem Buch entwickelten *erwerbsorientierten Grammatikunterricht.*

Das Buch hat Rezept- und Modellcharakter zugleich. Überlastete und noch wenig erfahrene Lehrer und Lehrerinnen können die Unterrichtsmodelle bedenkenlos als Rezepte übernehmen. Sie sind in der Praxis erprobt und funktionieren. Eine gewisse Anpassung an die Lernfähigkeit der Klasse geschieht dadurch, daß bei besseren Schülern die Schritte II oder III gekürzt oder auch einmal übersprungen werden können. Je nach Lernertyp kann der V. Schritt — die Bewußtmachung — auch schon nach dem III. Schritt erfolgen, und im III. und IV. Schritt kann schriftlich gearbeitet werden.

Weniger belastete oder experimentierfreudige Lehrer und Lehrerinnen können unter Beibehaltung der Gesamtsituation des I. Schrittes — der Demonstration — dessen Inhalte und damit die Vokabeln je nach Bedarf ändern. Änderungen in den nachfolgenden Schritten sind entsprechend vorzunehmen.

Nach der Durchnahme von 4–5 Unterrichtsmodellen werden die Unterrichtsschritte und die dabei verwendeten Strategien so geläufig, daß eigene Unterrichtseinheiten für in diesem Buch nicht aufgenommene grammatische Strukturen erstellt werden können.

Sprachlernpsychologische Begründung
und detaillierte Beschreibung
des erwerbsorientierten Grammatikunterrichts

Die verschiedenen Unterrichtsstrategien, die in den fünf Schritten der speziell für die Grammatikeinführung entwickelten Methode verwendet werden, sind im Unterricht erprobt, analysiert und getestet worden.

Unterrichtspraxis und -analyse sind jedoch biographischen Beschränktheiten und Zufälligkeiten unterworfen und müssen deshalb – um verallgemeinerungsfähig zu sein – auf Forschungserkenntnissen der Sprachlernpsychologie aufgebaut sein. Diese sprachlernpsychologische Begründung der in diesem Buch vorgeschlagenen *erwerbsorientierten* Methode zur Grammatikeinführung wird im folgenden vorgenommen.

I Demonstration

Welche Lehrerin und welcher Lehrer kennt nicht folgendes Unterrichtsproblem? Das *going to-future* soll zum ersten Mal eingeführt werden.

Verwendet der Lehrer das Lehrwerk *YES*[1], das exemplarisch für viele andere Lehrwerke stehe, wird er feststellen, daß die neue Struktur erstmals in Band 2, unit 4 erscheint und anhand fünf kurzer Texte, in denen englische Kinder Pläne für Wochenendausflüge machen, eingeführt wird. Alle Kurztexte sind durch fotografische Abbildungen der britischen Orte und Sehenswürdigkeiten, welche die Kinder aufsuchen wollen, illustriert. Die unit ist mit dem Titel *Making Plans* überschrieben, und die Situation wird durch den sprachlichen Vorspann *Dennis, Diana, Tom, Sandra and Wendy are making plans for the weekend* umrissen. Der erste Kurztext lautet dann *Dennis and Diana are going to visit London because they want to see the Crown Jewels in the Tower.*

Den Lehrbuchautoren gelingt es ganz offensichtlich, den von ihnen ausgesuchten Gebrauchswert des *going to-future* transparent zu machen: es wird verwendet, um auszudrücken, was jemand in der Zukunft zu tun »plant«.

Was soll aber mit den Texten konkret gemacht werden? Soll man sie vorlesen, soll eine Tonaufzeichnung vorgespielt werden, oder sollen die Schüler die Texte leise lesen?

Man holt sich Rat in der Lehrerhandreichung und erhält folgenden methodischen Hinweis:

---

[1] *YES – A New English Course.* Grundausgabe, Band 2. Dortmund: Lensing 1978, S. 33

Ehe die Schüler die Texte hören, sollte *going to* kurz eingeführt werden. Dann wird die Tonaufzeichnung vorgespielt, während die Schüler die Bilder betrachten und den Text mitlesen. Stehen Tonband oder Kassette nicht zur Verfügung, muß der Lehrer den Text vorlesen. Anschließend kann man einige Fragen zum Text stellen: *What are Dennis and Diana going to do? Why are they going to visit London?* Auf diese Weise läßt sich *going to* üben und festigen.[1]

Der Rat suchende Lehrer ist einigermaßen enttäuscht, denn genau das, wofür er Hilfe wollte – die Einführung der Struktur –, soll er »kurz« selbst vornehmen. Der Praktiker weiß zudem, daß nach einem einmaligen Vorspielen der Tonaufzeichnung – nachdem die neue Struktur erst fünfmal vorgesprochen wurde – die Lehrerfrage *What are Dennis and Diana going to do?* zu früh kommt. Die falsche Schüleräußerung *Dennis and Diana are going to do visit London* ist vorprogrammiert. Der Zwang zu einem verfrühten Produzieren der neuen Struktur führt zu dem bekannten, unterrichtsspezifischen Fehler.

Die Tatsache, daß die erste Einführung einer neuen Struktur dem Lehrer überlassen bleibt, ist jedoch kein Mangel des speziellen Lehrbuches *YES*, sondern liegt im Medium Lehrwerk im allgemeinen begründet. Lehrbuchtexte können nämlich eine reale Kommunikationssituation, in der ein lebender Sprecher mit Hilfe von Sprache, Gestik, Mimik und Blickkontakt direkt mit den Schülern kommuniziert, nicht ersetzen. Besonders in der Präsentationsphase, wenn die neue grammatische Struktur erstmals vorgeführt wird, erreicht man dann den größten Lerneffekt, wenn der Lehrer die Kommunikationssituation selbst aktiv gestaltet, die Sprache vorlebt und für die Schüler sinnlich erfahrbar werden läßt.

Diese Behauptung soll durch einen Rückgriff auf Erkenntnisse über den Mutterspracherwerb begründet werden. Zweifelsohne ist der Erwerb der Muttersprache etwas anderes als der schulische Fremdsprachenerwerb. Trotzdem wirken natürliche Erwerbsprinzipien über den Erstspracherwerb hinaus und sind auch noch unter den künstlichen Bedingungen des Fremdsprachenunterrichts wirksam, wenn sie nicht durch unüberlegte schulische Lerntechniken zugeschüttet werden.[2]

Heute glaubt man, daß der kindliche Spracherwerb durch das Zusammenspiel zwischen Mutter und Kind erfolgt.[3] Die Mutter oder eine andere Bezugsperson stellt schon vor dem Sprachbeginn des Kleinkindes durch routinehafte, regelmäßig wiederkehrende Handlungen und Situationen, z.B. beim Füttern, Saubermachen, Spielen und Liebkosen, ein stabiles Interaktionsmuster her. Das Kleinkind kommuniziert vorsprachlich ständig mit der Mutter, die durch ihre rituellen Handlungen für ein Verstehen aus der Situation heraus sorgt. Die Handlungen der Mutter werden für das Kleinkind so klar und voraussehbar, daß sie für das allmähliche

---

[1] *YES – A New English Course.* Lehrerhandreichungen, Band 2. Dortmund: Lensing 1978, S. L 33
[2] Wode, Henning: »Die Entwicklung des sprachlichen Hörens und seine Bedeutung für einen zeitgemäßen Deutschunterricht«, *Der Deutschunterricht* 5/90, S. 19–24, bes. S. 30 ff.
[3] Macnamara, J.: »The cognitive basis of language learning in infants«, *Psychological Review* 79, S. 1–13; Bruner, J.S.: *Child's talk.* New York: Norton 1983

Verständnis der sie begleitenden Sprache ein verläßliches Gerüst bilden. Das Kind benutzt also das sprachunabhängig gewonnene Sinnverstehen zum Verstehen von Sprache. Der Weg des Sprachverstehens geht somit nicht von Wort und Grammatik zur Bedeutung, sondern umgekehrt von der Bedeutung, d.h. dem Situationsverständnis, zum Wort und zur Grammatik.

Was läßt sich nun von den lernpsychologischen Forschungsergebnissen im Bereich des Muttterspracherwerbs für die erste Präsentation von Grammatikstrukturen im Fremdsprachenunterricht verwerten?

Wenn die Lernenden einer neuen grammatischen Struktur zum ersten Mal begegnen, wird von ihnen sprachlich sehr viel verlangt. Sie müssen sowohl die äußere Form als auch den Gebrauchswert, den Funktionsbereich und die Anwendungsmöglichkeiten eines ihnen bisher unbekannten sprachlichen Mittels verstehen. Das kann nur unter Bedingungen gelingen, die der Lehrer in der künstlichen Situation des Schulunterrichts selbst schaffen muß:

1. Der Lehrer muß eine Kommunikationssituation wählen, die für den Schüler völlig **klar** ist. Das Verstehen der neuen Struktur muß sich aus der Logik der Situation heraus eindeutig ergeben.

2. Die Kommunikationssituation muß so gewählt werden, daß die neue grammatische Struktur **angemessen** verwendet wird, d.h., die gewählte Situation muß typisch sein für den Strukturgebrauch.

3. Die Kommunikationssituation muß **sprachlich** so **ergiebig** sein, daß möglichst viele Sätze der gewünschten Sprachform — mindestens 10 bis 15 — routinehaft und in möglichst natürlicher Weise vorgesprochen werden können.

4. Die Präsentation muß **lebendig** sein. Je mehr Sinne der Schüler durch Mimik, Gestik, ausgeprägte Intonation und Anschauungsmaterial angesprochen werden, je verzweigter also die semantische Verarbeitung der neuen Struktur ist, desto größer ist die Aufmerksamkeit, und desto besser sind Verständnis und Behalten.

5. Die Präsentation muß **interessant** und **schülerorientiert** sein. Nur wenn der Inhalt des **Kommunizierten** an die Interessen, die Belange und Bedürfnisse der Schüler anknüpft, wird sich der Lernende angesprochen fühlen und innerlich beteiligen.

6. Der gewählte situative Rahmen muß **lernzielorientiert** sein, d.h., er darf nicht so weit gewählt werden, daß die neue Struktur von anderen Spracherscheinungen überlagert wird und die Schüler vom eigentlichen Sprachproblem abgelenkt werden.

Um die genannten sechs Bedingungen weitestgehend zu erfüllen, arbeitet das vorliegende Buch in der Demonstrationsphase mit einer Vielzahl von Textsorten wie Fragebögen, Tagebucheinträge, Schlagzeilen, Berichte, Erzählungen, Interviews, Schilderaufschriften, Stundenpläne, Vorschriften usw. Außerdem mit Grafiken wie Tabellen und Diagramme und mit Strichzeichnungen.

Wie der Lehrer die Schüler unter Verwendung der neuen Struktur anzusprechen hat, ist sprachlich genau vorformuliert.

II Verstehen und Reagieren

Wie wir gesehen haben, kommuniziert das Kleinkind schon vor dem Sprachbeginn in vielfacher Art mit seinen Bezugspersonen. Bereits in den 20er Jahren wiesen Clara und William Stern[1] nach, daß im Erstspracherwerb das Kind anfangs mehr versteht, als es sagen kann.

Roger Brown, ein führender Experte der Erforschung des Erstspracherwerbs, gab auf die Frage, wie die Eltern ihren Kindern das Erlernen der Sprache erleichtern können, folgenden Rat: »Believe that your child can understand more than he or she can say; and seek, above all, to communicate. (…) If you concentrate on communicating, everything else will follow.«[2]

Vereinzelte Fremdsprachendidaktiker zogen schon zu Beginn der 60er Jahre ihre Konsequenzen aus diesen Erkenntnissen über den Erstspracherwerb. Nämlich daß der Schüler Zeit braucht, um das neue Sprachmaterial in seiner Komplexität gründlich verarbeiten zu können. Eine verfrühte mündliche Verwendung verunsichert den Schüler, er macht Fehler, und der gewünschte Lerneffekt bleibt aus. F.L. Billows meinte schon 1961: »If the teacher tries to hurry the process, the learners may be uncertain of what to say, make mistakes, and lose confidence.«[3]

Man suchte nach Methoden, wie man die Sprachproduktion des Schülers zurückstellen und die Lernenden dadurch entlasten konnte, daß *vor* der Produktion fremdsprachlicher Äußerungen das Hör- und Situationsverstehen ausführlich trainiert wurde.

Ein methodischer Versuch bestand darin, zumindest im Anfangsunterricht weitgehend mit Bewegungsspielen zu operieren. In Palmers *English through actions*[4] reagierten die Schüler auf die Sprachäußerungen des Lehrers nicht verbal, sondern durch Handlungen. Sie wiesen ihr Hörverstehen durch die körperliche Ausführung von sprachlichen Kommandos nach, wie z.B. »take your neighbour's hand and shake it« oder »go to the blackboard and write your name, please«.

Ende der 70er Jahre, als sich Sprachlernpsychologen und Fremdsprachendidaktiker verstärkt der Fertigkeit des Hörverstehens zuwandten, wurde das Prinzip des *delayed oral practice* dann empirisch überprüft und besonders von J.J. Asher[5] zu der umfassenden Methode des *total physical response* ausgebaut.

[1] Stern, Clara/Stern, William: *Monographien über die seelische Entwicklung des Kindes.* Leipzig: Barth 1928, S. 165
[2] Brown, Roger: »Introduction«, in: Snow, C.E./Ferguson, C.A.: *Talking to Children.* Cambridge: University Press 1977, S. 26
[3] Billows, F.L.: *The Techniques of Language Teaching.* London: Longman 1961, S. 5
[4] Palmer, H.E./Palmer, D.: *English through actions.* London: Longman 1925/1958
[5] Asher, James J.: *Learning another language through actions: The complete teacher's guide book.* Los Gatos/CA: Sky Oaks Productions 1977

Ashers Unterrichtsbeispiele widerlegen zwar, daß der Lehrer, wie man anfänglich meinen könnte, sprachlich nur auf die Befehlsform beschränkt sei. Trotzdem sollte man eine Methode — wie unsere eigenen Unterrichtsexperimente nahelegen — nicht überstrapazieren und eine sprachliche Reaktion der Lernenden nicht zu lange hinauszögern. Die Schüler wollen im Dialog mit dem Lehrer sprachlich reagieren, und man muß eine geeignete Strategie finden, wie sie dies — ohne die neu eingeführte grammatische Struktur schon selbst verwenden zu müssen — tun können. Im zweiten Schritt der *erwerbsorientierten* Methode zur Einführung von Grammatikstrukturen benutzt der Lehrer deshalb die neue grammatische Struktur nur selbst und gibt den Schülern damit weitere Gelegenheit, das neue Sprachmittel hörend zu verstehen, zu internalisieren und die grammatische Regel intuitiv zu durchschauen und zu erfassen. Die vorgeschlagenen Dialoge ermöglichen es den Lernenden, sprachlich mit dem Lehrer zu kommunizieren und ihr Hör- und Situationsverständnis nur unter Verwendung ihnen schon bekannter Sprachmittel zu beweisen.

III und IV Reproduzieren und Produzieren

In der modernen Erstspracherwerbstheorie geht man davon aus, daß Lerner der Muttersprache ihre Sprache weder durch einen bewußten intellektuellen Prozeß erlernen noch durch eine Regelvorgabe, sondern durch ein mentales, angeborenes Spracherwerbsprogramm, das ihnen nicht bewußt ist.

Ohne die Annahme eines solchen Programmes ließe sich das Wunder der Sprache nicht erklären, daß nämlich Menschen mit den Strukturen ihrer Muttersprache meisterlich umzugehen und Regeln anzuwenden lernen, deren sie sich nicht bewußt sind und die sie nicht verbalisieren, geschweige denn erklären können.

Ohne die Annahme eines solchen genetischen Programmes ließe sich auch nicht erklären, weshalb der Erstspracherwerb aufgrund von unumkehrbaren Entwicklungssequenzen erfolgt, die sich unabhängig von der jeweiligen sprachlichen Umgebung entfalten.

Der amerikanische Sprachwissenschaftler Noam Chomsky und seine Schule weisen die auf dem Verhaltensforscher B.F. Skinner[1] basierende behavioristische Spracherwerbstheorie zurück, nach der Sprachenlernen durch die Verbindung eines sprachlichen oder außersprachlichen Reizes (*stimulus*) mit einer darauf folgenden sprachlichen Reaktion (*response*) erfolgt. Nach Skinner wird die Verbindung zwischen Stimulus und Response dadurch gefestigt, daß dem Response eine Verstärkung (*reinforcement*) folgt. Erwünschtes Verhalten wird also durch Reinforcement verstärkt — unerwünschtes Verhalten erfährt keine Verstärkung, wodurch sich die Verbindung zwischen Stimulus und Response immer mehr festigt.

---

[1] Skinner, B.F.: *Verbal Behaviour*. New York: Meredith 1957

Skinner bezeichnet die Herstellung einer festen Verbindung zwischen Stimulus und Response durch wiederholte Verstärkung als *operant conditioning* und erachtet das Erlernen der Muttersprache durch ein Kind als ein Beispiel dafür. Chomsky[1] lehnte Skinners behavioristische Theorie in einem vernichtenden Artikel völlig ab, und zwar mit der Begründung, daß sie an Tierexperimenten entwickelt wurde und sich auf menschliches Verhalten nicht übertragen ließe. Nach Chomsky und seiner Schule ist menschliches Sprachverhalten kreativ und nicht vorhersagbar. Der Spracherwerb besteht im Erwerb des Regelsystems, das den vom Kleinkind aufgenommenen sprachlichen Daten zugrunde liegt.

Nicht nur die Tatsache, daß der Erstspracherwerb bestimmten, unumkehrbaren Entwicklungssequenzen folgt, sondern auch die Schnelligkeit des Spracherwerbs von Kindern und ihre Fähigkeit, Sätze zu erzeugen und zu verstehen, die sie zuvor noch nie gehört oder produziert haben, führten Chomsky zu der Annahme eines dem Menschen angeborenen Spracherwerbsmechanismus (*language acquisition device,* kurz LAD).

Dieser LAD zeichnet sich durch spezifische Eigenschaften aus, die so für andere kognitive Bereiche nicht gelten und den Muttersprachlerner dazu befähigen, aus einer begrenzten Menge sprachlicher Daten unbewußt Regeln abzuleiten, die es ihm erlauben, eine unbegrenzte Menge von Sätzen zu erzeugen und zu verstehen: »Every ›theory of learning‹ that is worth considering incorporates an innateness hypothesis.«[2]

In seiner ursprünglichen generativen Sprachtheorie vertrat Chomsky die Vorstellung, daß der Spracherwerbsmechanismus dem Kind eine Reihe von möglichen grammatischen Regelsystemen automatisch anbietet und daß das Kind lediglich die Aufgabe hat, aufgrund des verfügbaren Inputs diejenige Grammatik auszuwählen, die mit dem angebotenen Sprachmaterial verträglich ist. Spracherwerb bedeutet nach dieser Theorie Regelsysteme auswählen und bewerten, d.h. Hypothesen testen.

In den letzten zehn Jahren veränderte Chomsky seine in den 60er Jahren begründete generative Sprachtheorie selbst[3], und andere Spracherwerbsforscher und Sprachwissenschaftler[4] nahmen weitere Veränderungen vor. Die problematische Annahme des hypothesentestenden Sprachlerners, d.h. des Kindes, das ganze Regelsysteme ansetzen und nachträglich testen würde, ließ sich mit empirischen Spracherwerbsergebnissen nicht vereinbaren und wird heute zurückgewiesen. Untersuchungen zum Verlauf der Sprachentwicklung bei Kindern zeigten, daß der Erwerb der Sprachstrukturen nicht so sehr ein Prozeß des Auswählens, sondern

---

[1] Chomsky, Noam: »A Review of B.F. Skinner's ›Verbal Behaviour‹«, *Language* 35 (Heft 1), S. 26–58, 1958
[2] Chomsky, Noam: *Reflections on Language.* New York: Pantheon 1975, S. 13
[3] Chomsky, Noam: *Lectures on government and binding.* Dordrecht: Foris 1981
Chomsky, Noam: *Knowledge of language.* New York: Praeger 1986
[4] Rizzi, L.: *Issues in Italian syntax.* Dordrecht: Foris 1982; Felix, S.: *Cognition and language growth.* Dordrecht: Foris 1987

eher des Konstruierens einer Grammatik ist.[1] Bei allen Veränderungen sind jedoch die Grundvorstellungen der generativen Sprachtheorie, insbesondere die mentalistische Sicht der Sprachfähigkeit und die damit verbundenen, behavioristische Theorien widerlegenden Annahmen beibehalten worden.

Fremdsprachendidaktiker, die die Unterschiede zwischen Mutterspracherwerb und schulischem Fremdsprachenerwerb nicht deutlich auseinandergehalten hatten, entwickelten Unterrichtsmethoden, die sich sowohl auf Skinners als auch auf Chomskys Theorie stützten.

Skinners behavioristische Spracherwerbstheorie führte zu der Annahme, daß auch im schulischen Fremdsprachenerwerb die Verbindung von sprachlichem oder nichtsprachlichem Reiz mit einer sprachlichen Reaktion so häufig wiederholt und bekräftigt werden solle, bis eine feste Verbindung hergestellt sei. Das Erlernen der Sprache erfolge dabei weitgehend unbewußt, imitativ und automatisch. Die Aufgabe des Lehrers bestand darin, Lehrmaterialien und möglichst kurzschrittige Übungssequenzen anzubieten, die durch imitatives Lernen zum Aufbau von Sprachgewohnheiten führten.

Besonders das in der audio-lingualen Methode gängige Verfahren des *pattern practice,* das Einschleifen von Strukturen zum Zwecke der Habitualisierung und mechanische Drillübungen, bevorzugt im Sprachlabor, fußten auf der behavioristischen Theorie.

Die fremdsprachendidaktische Reaktion auf Chomskys mentalistische Theorie war widersprüchlich.

Zum einen führte Chomskys ursprüngliche Theorie des regelgesteuerten Mutterspracherwerbs zu der Annahme, bewußtes Lernen im Fremdsprachenunterricht erleichtere den Lernprozeß. Besonders der Grammatikerwerb sei durch lediglich unbewußtes Üben nicht gewährleistet. Den Schülern müßten Regeln angeboten werden, die erklärten, wie bestimmte sprachliche Erscheinungen funktionieren, um dadurch kognitives Lernen zu ermöglichen: »Ein optimaler Übungseffekt kommt nur zustande, wenn der Lernende Sprachprozesse vollzieht und zugleich die Systematik kennt, aus der heraus diese Prozesse richtig/falsch sind.«[2] Verfasser von Grammatikdidaktiken betonten aber nachdrücklich, daß das Bewußtmachen von Grammatikregeln keine Rückkehr bedeute »zum alten Regelkult des grammatisierenden Unterrichts; sondern nur die Stützung des Sprachgefühls und der Analogiebildung durch Einsicht«.[3]

Chomskys Theorie des dem Menschen angeborenen Spracherwerbsmechanismus (LAD) führte andererseits zu dem fremdsprachendidaktischen Postulat, die Grammatikarbeit aus dem Fremdsprachenunterricht ganz zu verbannen und es

[1] Clashen, Harald: *Spracherwerb in der Kindheit.* Tübingen: Narr 1982
[2] Hüllen, Werner: *Linguistik und Englischunterricht.* Heidelberg: Quelle & Meyer 1971, S. 102
[3] Hinz, Klaus: *Grammatik im Unterricht.* Moderner Englischunterricht: Arbeitshilfen für die Praxis 8. Hannover: Schroedel; Dortmund: Lensing 1977, S. 26

den Schülern selbst zu überlassen, die Regeln der fremdsprachlichen Grammatik intuitiv zu erfassen.[1]

Für Stephan Krashen z.B. ist der wichtigste Faktor beim Mutter- und Fremdspracherwerb der verständliche *input*. Grammatik wird dann gelernt, wenn der Lernende ständig Sprache hört, die er, über die Logik der Situation vermittelt, versteht. Das situative Verstehen alleine setze das angeborene mentale Spracherwerbsprogramm in Gang. Bewußte Einsicht in die Sprachstrukturen würden den eigentlichen Erwerb der Fremdsprache im Schulunterricht nicht fördern, sie könnte nur als *monitor* fungieren, indem der Lernende seine Sprachäußerung nachträglich auf die Richtigkeit hin überprüft und ggf. korrigiert.[2]

Sowohl Chomskys als auch Krashens Vorstellungen sind nicht unwidersprochen geblieben.

Chomsky begründete seine Theorie des angeborenen LAD u.a. mit der Behauptung, daß die Sprache, die dem die Muttersprache erwerbenden Kind zugesprochen wird, meist aus begrenztem und defektem Sprachmaterial bestehe und daß das Kind trotz dieses mangelhaften Sprachinputs die Sprache erlerne.[3]

Experten des Mutterspracherwerbs, die ein umfangreiches Dialogmaterial zwischen Mutter und Kind gesammelt und analysiert haben, kamen jedoch zu dem Ergebnis, daß die Bezugspersonen nicht nur versuchen, eine völlig durchsichtige Kommunikationssituation herzustellen und eine verständliche Nachricht zu vermitteln, sondern auch bemüht sind, den Kindern artikulatorisch korrekte und syntaktisch zwar reduzierte, aber korrekte und transparente Sprachstrukturen zu bieten: »The mother's input and feedback is so adapted in its temporal and structural relations to filial speech that it exhibits the analytic, pattern-abstracting, word-class defining, and syntactic features that are needed to help the child analyse the regularities underlying the strings of sounds she hears.«[4]

Intuitiv betätigen sich Eltern als Sprachlehrer ihrer Kinder, indem sie nicht nur langsamer, deutlicher und redundanter als normal sprechen, sondern den lernenden Kindern deren Sprachvermögen gemäß transparente syntaktische Strukturen anbieten, die dem Kind verdeutlichen, welche Worte im Satz wohin gehören. Die Elternsprache – schon Siebenjährige beherrschen sie, wenn sie zu kleineren Kindern sprechen – ist also so beschaffen, daß das Kind seinen LAD darauf anwenden kann. Erst diese spezifische Elternsprache ermöglicht den Mutterspracherwerb, zumindest aber erleichtert und fördert sie ihn.

Untersuchungen von Dialogen zwischen Mutter und Kind zeigten weiterhin, daß der Mutterspracherwerb eine Gemeinschaftsarbeit darstellt und nur in gemein-

[1] Dulay, Heidi/Burt, Marina/Krashen, Stephan: *Language two.* New York, Oxford: OUP 1982

[2] Krashen, Stephan: *Second Language Acquisition and Second Language Learning.* Oxford: Pergamon Press 1981 und *Principles and Practice in Second Language Acquisition.* Oxford: Pergamon Press 1982

[3] Chomsky, Noam: *Reflections on language.* New York: Pantheon 1975, S. 10 und 22

[4] Moerk, E.L.: »Analytic, synthetic, abstracting and word-class-defining aspects of verbal mother-child interactions«, *Journal of Psycholinguistic Research,* Heft 14/3, 1985, S. 265

samer Anstrengung zwischen Bezugsperson und Kind erfolgt. Im Dialog mit der Bezugsperson versucht das lernende Kind, seine Worte richtig zu setzen, und erfährt bei seiner unbewußten Hypothesenbildung über die Sprachstruktur ständig Rückmeldung und Hilfestellung durch die Mutter. Die Mutter oder eine andere Bezugsperson greift die sprachlichen Äußerungen des Kindes geduldig auf, versucht sie zu verstehen und spielt sie dem Kind so zurück, daß es die neue Sprachstruktur nicht nur situativ, sondern auch struktural begreifen kann. Kindliche Äußerungen werden sprachlich bestätigt, ggf. korrigiert, weitergeführt und expandiert, so daß ein Lernfortschritt möglich wird.[1]

Mutterspracherwerb beruht damit nicht nur auf verständlichem Input, wie Krashen postuliert, sondern auch auf einer Art von dialogischem Unterricht, an dem Mutter *und* Kind aktiv beteiligt sind, ohne daß sich die Mutter ihrer Lehrtätigkeit bewußt werden muß.

Empirische Beobachtungen an Kindern, die ihre Muttersprache erlernen, zeigen zudem, daß lernende Kinder die Sprache spielerisch üben, d.h. spielerisch *pattern practice* betreiben. Besonders wenn Kinder alleine sind oder kurz bevor sie einschlafen, »spielen« sie mit Sprachstrukturen. John Holt z.B., ein Erforscher von Kindersprache, machte folgende Beobachtung an seiner zweieinhalbjährigen Tochter Lisa: »Much of her talk might be called experiments with grammar, that is exercises in putting together words in the way that people around her put them together. She makes word patterns, sentences, that sound like the sentences she hears. What do they mean? Often they do not mean anything, and are not meant to mean anything.«[2]

Bei diesen spielerischen Sprachübungen ist die Sprache also nicht Mittel zur Kommunikation oder zum Ausdruck eigener Bedürfnisse, sondern die Sprache selbst wird zum interessanten Gegenstand. Das lernende Kind versucht, die Sprachstruktur zu durchschauen, damit es Wörter und Ausdrücke wie Bauklötzchen neu kombinieren kann. Unbewußt arbeitet es an der Ausbildung von produktiven Sprachregeln.

Methodische Vorschläge, schulische Fremdsprachenlerner einfach mit situativ verständlichem und ergiebigem Sprachmaterial zu versorgen, d.h., sie in ein *language bath* zu stecken, setzen somit nicht nur undifferenziert den Mutter- mit dem schulischen Fremdspracherwerb gleich, sondern übersehen auch die geschilderten spezifischen Voraussetzungen für die Aktivierung des unbewußten Erwerbsmechanismus beim Erlernen der Muttersprache.

Die Strategien des III. und IV. Schrittes der in diesem Buch verwendeten Methode zur Einführung von Grammatikstrukturen sind einerseits so gestaltet, daß sie den beim Mutterspracherwerb wirksamen unbewußten Erwerbsstrategien zuarbeiten,

[1] Crystal, David: *Listen to your child. A parent's guide to children's language.* Harmondsworth: Penguin 1986, S. 113ff.
[2] Holt, John: *How Children Learn.* Harmondsworth: Penguin 1970, S. 71

zumindest aber ihnen nicht entgegenstehen. Andererseits berücksichtigen sie die Unterschiede zwischen mutter- und fremdsprachlichem Lehr- und Lernprozeß. Während die Erlernung der Erstsprache ein natürlicher Prozeß der Entwicklung und Lebensbewältigung ist, ist die Erlernung der Fremdsprache für den Lerner nicht von existentieller Bedeutung, denn die fremde Sprache ist zur unmittelbaren Lebensbewältigung nicht notwendig. Der schulische Fremdsprachenunterricht hat im Vergleich zur natürlichen Erwerbssituation weitere ungünstige Bedingungen: Die Hör- und Sprechzeit ist begrenzt, eine ganze Klasse muß sich mit einem Lehrer begnügen – im Muttersprach- und natürlichen Zweitspracherwerb stehen für einen Lernenden meist mehrere »Lehrer« zur Verfügung –, und schließlich kann die im Klassenzimmer vorgestellte Welt die reale Welt der Zielsprachenkultur nicht ersetzen.

Die Kunst des Fremdsprachendidaktikers besteht nun darin, unter den ungünstigen Bedingungen der Schule Lehr- und Lernstrategien zu erfinden, die sowohl die natürlichen Sprachlernfähigkeiten als auch die kognitiven Fähigkeiten der Schüler – die sie von dem die Muttersprache erlernenden Kleinkind unterscheiden – ausnutzen.

Die Strategien des III. und IV. Schrittes des *erwerbsorientierten* Grammatikunterrichts weisen demnach folgende Charakteristika auf:

Reproduzieren (III)

1. Der Lehrer kommuniziert mit den Schülern über einen Inhalt, der sie über das bloß sprachliche Ziel hinaus interessiert.
2. Im Dialog mit den Schülern spielt der Lehrer den Lernenden die neue grammatische Struktur zu.
3. In ihrem Response verwenden die Schüler dieselbe Struktur erstmals selbst, indem sie die Lehreräußerung entweder reproduzieren oder ihren sprachlichen Fähigkeiten und ihren Interessen gemäß durch Verwendung anderer Wörter leicht verändern.
4. Die Schüler haben die Möglichkeit, nach unbekannten Wörtern zu fragen und ihre Äußerungen ihren Bedürfnissen nach zu variieren. Dadurch werden sie nicht auf den vorprogrammierten Wortschatz beschränkt und erleben die Sprache als Mittel zur Situationsbewältigung.
5. Mit Hilfe eines natürlichen Lehrerechos nimmt der Lehrer die Schüleräußerungen noch einmal auf, wodurch diese entweder bestätigt, ohne Zurechtweisung korrigiert oder expandiert und weitergeführt werden.
6. Die Schüler erhalten Dialogmuster und *sentence switchboards,* die sie in die Lage versetzen, die strukturbildenden Elemente des neuen Sprachmittels zu erkennen. Dadurch können sie neben der Gebrauchssicherheit ein Strukturgefühl entwickeln, das sie zur Bildung neuer Sätze befähigt.

Produzieren (IV)

1. Die Schüler verwenden die neue grammatische Struktur zum ersten Mal selbständig ohne Hilfe des Lehrers.
2. In Gruppen- oder Partnergesprächen wird das neue Sprachmittel benutzt. Der Lehrer hört nur zu und überprüft die sprachliche Korrektheit der Schüleräußerungen.
3. Die Schüler verwenden das neue Sprachmittel zur personen- und sachbezogenen Kommunikation: sie geben über sich persönlich Auskunft, sie befragen sich gegenseitig, sie treffen untereinander Vereinbarungen, sie sprechen über ihre Lebenssituation und ihre Gewohnheiten, sie spielen miteinander und führen Rollenspiele durch. Dadurch erfahren die Schüler, daß man mit der fremden Sprache und dem neuen Sprachmittel konkret etwas anfangen kann, sie erleben die Fremdsprache als ein echtes Kommunikationsmittel.

V Bewußtmachung

Das Erlernen einer Fremdsprache in der Schule stellt den Erwerb einer komplexen Fertigkeit dar. Der deutsche Fremdsprachendidaktiker Wolfgang Butzkamm weist unter Aufarbeitung der Ergebnisse der Fertigkeitspsychologie nach, daß beim Erwerb komplexer Fertigkeiten **Erklären**, d.h. Bewußtmachung, immer mit beteiligt ist: »Je weniger die zu erwerbenden Fertigkeiten mit naturgegebenen Lebensbedingungen des Menschen verwurzelt sind, desto mehr wird auch der Intellekt an ihrem Erlernen beteiligt. Die Unterscheidung von eher naturwüchsigen und eher künstlichen Fertigkeiten drängt sich auf. Sie hat damit zu tun, wieviel an den Leistungen genetisch vorprogrammiert ist und damit von vornherein unbewußt ablaufen kann bzw. wieviel an Üben und bewußt-rationalem Lernen hinzukommen kann.«[1]

Während der Erwerb der Muttersprache eher eine natürliche Fertigkeit darstellt, die sich allerdings ohne eine sprechende und zum Dialog bereite Umwelt nicht entwickeln kann, kommt der schulische Fremdsprachenerwerb eher der Ausbildung einer künstlichen Fertigkeit gleich, die zwar auf natürlichen Spracherwerbsmechanismen aufbaut, aber eines hohen Trainings- und Bewußtmachungsanteils bedarf. Fertigkeitspsychologen sind der Ansicht, daß zum Erwerb von komplexen Fertigkeiten bewußte Einsichten notwendig sind, daß anfangs bewußt und gezielt geübt wird, daß diese Einsichten jedoch mit wachsendem Können ins Unbewußte absinken, damit sich ein selbständiger Mechanismus und Automatismus herausbilden kann.

---

[1] Butzkamm, Wolfgang: *Psycholinguistik des Fremdsprachenunterrichts.* Tübingen: R. Franke 1989, S. 77

Die fertigkeitspsychologischen Forschungsergebnisse haben im Konzept der in diesem Buch vorgeschlagenen Methode zur Einführung von Grammatik folgenden Niederschlag gefunden:

1. Die Unterrichtsmodelle sind dem kommunikativen Ansatz verpflichtet, d.h., es wird eher mitteilungs- als sprachbezogen kommuniziert, und die mit Hilfe der grammatischen Struktur intendierte Äußerungsabsicht steht im Vordergrund. Trotzdem halten sich die Modelle an die traditionelle grammatische Progression und nicht, wie viele Kommunikationsdidaktiker gefordert haben[1], an eine pragmalinguistische. Die Nachteile einer auf Sprechakttypen basierenden Progression sind vielerorts beschrieben worden.[2] Es existiert bis heute weder eine einigermaßen gesicherte Taxonomie von Sprechakttypen noch eine ausreichend abgesicherte Zuordnung linguistischer Mittel zu Sprechakttypen. Außerdem liegt dem Vorschlag einer pragmalinguistischen Progression »ein fundamentales Mißverständnis über Grammatikerwerb« zugrunde: »Eine pragmalinguistische Reihung würde ja das generative Prinzip der Satzerzeugung eher verdecken.«[3]

2. Die ersten vier Schritte der Methode sind so gestaltet, daß der Schüler nicht nur die Situation, sondern auch die sprachliche Struktur durchschaut, um damit produktive Satzerzeugungsregeln entwickeln zu können.

3. Im V. Schritt, dem Schritt der »Bewußtmachung«, werden der semantisch-pragmatische Gehalt und der strukturale Aufbau der neuen grammatischen Struktur, die den Schülern in den Schritten zuvor schon transparent gemacht wurden, in Regeln gefaßt. Diese späte Regelfassung hat den Vorteil, daß die Schüler schon eine genügend große Spracherfahrung gemacht und ein gewisses Problembewußtsein entwickelt haben.

Die Regeln werden von den Schülern unter Mithilfe des Lehrers erarbeitet. Dies ist lernpsychologisch begründet, da **Selbstgefundenes** besser haftenbleibt und eher zum Transfer auf verwandte Probleme zur Verfügung steht.[4]

---

[1] Piepho, H.E.: *Kommunikative Kompetenz als übergeordnetes Lernziel im Englischunterricht.* Dornburg-Frickhofen: Frankonius 1974

[2] Z.B. Mindt, Dieter: »Probleme des pragmalinguistischen Ansatzes in der Fremdsprachendidaktik«, *Die Neueren Sprachen,* Heft 3/4, S. 340–356

[3] Butzkamm, Wolfgang, a.a.O., S. 230

[4] Göller, H.: »Lernpsychologische und kognitive Grammatikarbeit im Französischunterricht«, *Praxis des neusprachlichen Unterrichts,* 4/1982, S. 401–408

Unterrichtsmodelle: grammatische Strukturen

Adverbs of manner

What sort of person are you?

Name: ....

1. Are you good at entertaining people? Do you tell jokes
   ☐ well?   ☐ badly?

2. How do you usually dress?
   ☐ simply, in old clothes   ☐ fashionably?
     you feel happy in?

3. How do you usually talk to your parents?
   ☐ politely, in a friendly way?   ☐ rudely, often angrily?

4. How do you normally react to other people's suggestions?
   ☐ critically?   ☐ with interest?

5. How do you react when someone criticises you?
   ☐ angrily?   ☐ quietly: you listen and think about it

6. Do you normally work?
   ☐ hard?   ☐ not too hard?

7. Do you usually work
   ☐ fast?   ☐ slowly?
   ☐ carefully?   ☐ not very carefully?

Now look at the answers and see how many points you have got.
Points:
1. well – 2; badly – 1
2. simply, in old clothes you feel happy in – 2; fashionably – 1
3. in a friendly, polite way – 2; rudely, often angrily – 1
4. critically – 1; with interest – 2
5. angrily – 1; quietly: you listen and think about it – 2
6. hard – 2; not too hard – 1
7. fast – 1; slowly – 1; carefully – 2; not very carefully – 1

11–14 points: Very good. You seem to be a well-balanced, cheerful sort of person who is fun to be with.
7–10 points: Not bad, but perhaps there are some things you should think about.

I Demonstration

Legen Sie die Folie auf den Tageslichtprojektor und lesen Sie die Fragen vor. Sie werden aber noch nicht beantwortet. Der Auswertungsteil (*Points*) bleibt noch zugedeckt.

L: Look. This is a questionnaire. You can answer the questions and find out what sort of person you are.

First I'll read the questions to you. Tell me if there's anything you don't understand. We'll answer the questions later. Now what's the first question: Are you good at entertaining people? Do you tell jokes well or badly? And the second one: How do you usually dress: simply...? usw.

II Verstehen und Reagieren

Fragebogen ausfüllen
Teilen Sie an jeden Schüler den Fragebogen ohne den Auswertungsteil aus. Gemeinsam wird der Fragebogen ausgefüllt. Der Auswertungsteil auf der Folie bleibt noch zugedeckt.

L: Let's fill it in now. Look at the first question: Are you good at entertaining people? Do you tell jokes well or badly? Tick the right answer (✔).
Now number two: How...?
usw.

III Reproduzieren

Fragebogen auswerten
Der Auswertungsteil wird nun aufgedeckt, und die Punkte werden zusammengezählt. Beantworten Sie zuerst die jeweilige Frage für sich selbst, bevor Sie die Lernenden nach ihren Einträgen fragen.

L: Now let's see how many points we've all got. What about the first question: I tell jokes badly. So I only get one point. What about you?
S1: I tell jokes well.
L: So you get 2 points. Write it down.
S2: I tell jokes...
usw.
L: Now the second question: I usually dress simply, in old clothes I feel happy in. So I get 2 points. What about you?
S2: I usually dress...
usw.

IV Produzieren

Fragebogen auswerten
Schüler und Lehrer tauschen untereinander die Fragebögen aus und lesen die ihnen vorliegenden Eintragungen vor.

L: Give your questionnaire to someone else.
I've got (S1)'s. Let's see what sort of person she is.
She tells jokes badly.
(S1), whose have you got?

S1: (S2)'s.

L: Read (S2)'s answer to the first question, please.

S1: (S2) tells jokes well.

L: Go on, (S2).

S2: (S3) tells jokes badly.

S3: (S4) tells jokes...
usw.

Nachdem einige Schüler zu Wort gekommen sind, werden in der gleichen Weise die Einträge zu den restlichen Fragen vorgelesen.

V Bewußtmachung

Die Regel wird zum Teil von den Lernenden erarbeitet, indem sie zunächst die Grundform der Adverbien herausfinden.
Lesen Sie die auf der Folie erscheinenden Adverbien vor und stellen Sie sie in einer Liste zusammen.

L: Look at all these words that tell us how people do things: well, badly, simply, fashionably, politely, in a friendly way, rudely, angrily, critically, with interest, quietly, hard, fast, carefully, slowly.
We call words like these adverbs.
How do we form adverbs? Look at the adverb bad. Which word does that come from?

S1: Bad.

L: Yes. The adverb badly comes from the adjective bad. Get together in groups and find out which adjectives all these adverbs come from. You can use your dictionaries.

Lösungen:
well – good, badly – bad, simply – simple, fashionably – fashionable, politely – polite, in a friendly way – friendly, rudely – rude, angrily – angry, critically – critical, with interest – interested, quietly – quiet, hard – hard, fast – fast, carefully – careful, slowly – slow.

Erklären Sie nun die Regelbildung.

Most adverbs are formed by adding »ly« to the adjective: bad, polite, rude, critical, quiet, careful, slow.

Adjectives which end in »le« change their endings to »y«: simple, fashionable.

Adjectives ending in »y« change their endings to »i«: angry, (happy, easy).

Some adverbs look the same as the adjectives: hard, fast.

The adverb from »good« is »well«.

The adverb from »friendly« is »in a friendly way«.

Sometimes we use »with«: with interest (difficulty).

Adverbs of time and place: position

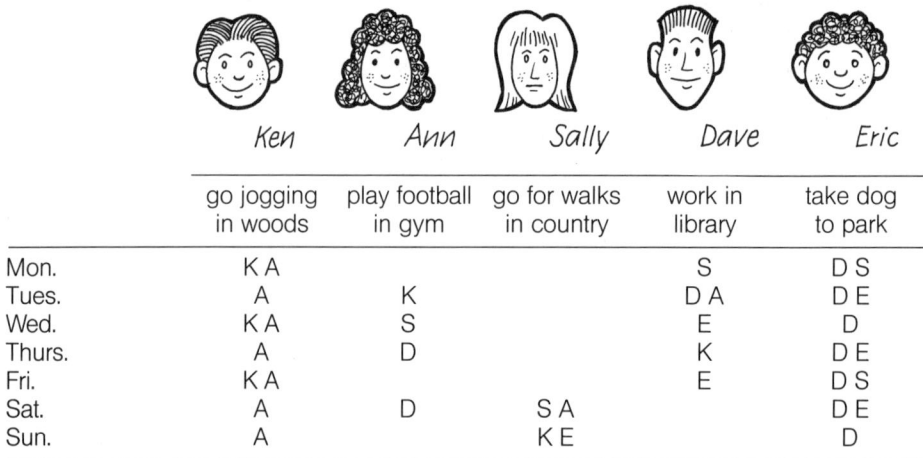

	Ken	Ann	Sally	Dave	Eric
	go jogging in woods	play football in gym	go for walks in country	work in library	take dog to park
Mon.	K A			S	D S
Tues.	A	K		D A	D E
Wed.	K A	S		E	D
Thurs.	A	D		K	D E
Fri.	K A			E	D S
Sat.	A	D	S A		D E
Sun.	A		K E		D

I Demonstration

Führen Sie die Folie ein, indem Sie kurz über Freizeitbeschäftigungen sprechen.
  L: What do you do in your spare time?
Beschreiben Sie nun die Freizeitaktivitäten von Ken und Ann. Deuten Sie dabei zuerst auf ihre Aktivitäten, dann auf den betreffenden Tag.
  L: Let's see what all these people do in their spare time. (Deuten Sie auf das Symbol für Ken.) Look, »K« stands for Ken. Ken goes jogging in the woods on Mondays, Wednesdays and Fridays.
    He plays football in the gym on Tuesdays. He goes for walks in the country on Sundays and he works in the library on Thursdays.
    What about Ann? What does she do in her spare time? She goes jogging in the woods every day. She goes…
    usw.

II Verstehen und Reagieren

Geheime Auswahl
Anhand Ihrer Beschreibungen versuchen die Lernenden herauszufinden, über welche der abgebildeten Personen Sie reden.
  L: Listen. Do you know who I'm talking about? He takes his dog to the park every day.

28

S1: Dave.

L: That's right. Listen again: These girls go for walks in the country at weekends.

S2: Sally and Ann.

usw.

Das Ratespiel wird schwieriger, wenn Sie für eine Person mehrere Aktivitäten angeben. Je nach Leistungsstand der Klasse kann auch die Struktur *he/she doesn't…* verwendet werden, z.B.

L: This person goes jogging in the woods on Fridays and works in the library on Tuesdays.

S1: Ann.

L: That's right. Listen again: This person goes for walks in the country at weekends. He doesn't play football.

S2: Eric.

usw.

Das Ratespiel kann auch als Mannschaftswettbewerb organisiert werden.

III Reproduzieren

Information erfragen und erteilen
Die Freizeitaktivitäten von jeweils einer der abgebildeten Personen werden beschrieben.

L: Let's see what (Sally) does in her spare time. She plays football in the gym on Wednesdays. What else?

S1: She goes for walks in the country on Saturdays/at weekends.

S2: She…

usw.

L: And Dave? He plays football in the gym on Thursdays and Saturdays. What else?

S1: He works…

usw.

IV Produzieren

Information erfragen und erteilen
Die Schüler befragen sich gegenseitig über die eigene Freizeitgestaltung. Schreiben Sie folgendes Satzmuster als Hilfestellung an:

I (play/…) in/at… (on Mondays/at the weekend).

L: Let's talk about what we do in our spare time. For instance, I go for walks in the woods at weekends. What about you? (Deuten Sie als Sprechimpuls auf das angeschriebene Muster und ermutigen Sie die Lernenden, nach unbekanntem Wortschatz zu fragen bzw. zu suchen.)

S1:   I play chess at the youth club on Fridays.

S2:   I…

     usw.

V Bewußtmachung

Im Englischen stehen Ortsadverbien vor Zeitadverbien. Als Merkhilfe für die Regel »Ort vor Zeit« (*place before time*) kann auf die alphabetische Reihenfolge der Buchstaben aufmerksam gemacht werden:

	place	before	time
	(Ort	vor	Zeit)
Keith goes jogging	in the woods		on Mondays.
Ann goes for walks	in the country		at weekends.

Any, anything, anybody, anywhere

I Demonstration

Führen Sie das Thema durch ein kurzes Gespräch über *camping* ein.

L: Do any of you go camping? Do you like it? Where did you go the last time? Who did you go with?

usw.

Legen Sie die Folie auf den Tageslichtprojektor.

L: When you first arrive at a camp site you need a lot of information, don't you? Look at these people. It's Nicola's, Colin's, Robert's and Sue's first day at this camp site, so they're asking a lot of questions.

(Schreiben Sie die Fragen und Antworten während Ihres Vortrags in zwei Spalten mit den Überschriften *Questions* und *Answers* auf. Unterstreichen Sie dabei *any, anything, anybody, anywhere*.)

Nicola asks, »Are there any shops here?«

The woman in the office tells her, »Well, there aren't any here, but there are some in the village.«

Then Nicola asks, »Do you know anything about buses to town?«

The woman tells her, »Sorry, I don't know anything about buses at all.«

Then Colin wants to know, »Can we buy stamps anywhere round here?«

The woman tells him, »We haven't any, but there's a post office in the village.«

Then he asks, »Can we get <u>anything</u> to eat here?«
She says, »No, you can't get <u>anything</u> on the camp site, but there's a café across the road.«
Then Robert asks, »Have you <u>any</u> information about this area?«
The woman tells him, »Sorry, I haven't <u>anything</u> at the moment.«
Sue is asking questions, too. She asks, »Does <u>anybody</u> know where the nearest phone box is?«
Tony tells her, »In the village.«
Then she asks, »Has <u>anybody</u> got change for a pound note?«

II Verstehen und Reagieren

Alternativantworten: Information erfragen und erteilen
Die gleichen Fragen, die in der I. Phase gestellt wurden, werden nun von Maria an ihre Freunde gerichtet. Die Lernenden sollen von zwei Alternativantworten die richtige wählen. Die Aufgabe wird schwieriger, wenn Sie Ihre angeschriebenen Sätze abdecken.

L: When Nicola, Colin, Robert and Sue go back to their tent Maria has a lot of questions, too.
She asks, »Are there any shops here?«
Colin says, »I think so.«
Nicola tells her, »No, there aren't any here.« Who is right?

S1: Nicola.

L: Yes. There aren't any on the camp site, but there are some in the village. (Wiederholen Sie jedesmal die richtige Antwort.)
Then Maria asks, »Do they know anything about buses to town?«
Sue says, »I think they've got a time-table.«
Robert tells her, »No, they don't know anything about buses.« Who is right?

S2: Robert.

L: Yes. They don't know anything…
Next Maria wants to know, »Can I buy stamps anywhere round here?«
Colin tells her, »They haven't any here.«
Nicola says, »There's a post office in the village.« Who is right?

S3: Both.

L: Yes. They haven't any here, but…
Then Maria says, »I'm hungry. Can we get anything to eat here?«
Robert tells her, »There isn't anything here.«
Sue says, »I think there's a café on the camp site.« Who is right?

S4: Robert.

L: Yes. There isn't anything on the camp site, but there's a café across the road.
Maria's next question is, »Have they any information about this area?«

32

Colin tells her, »They haven't anything at the moment.«
Nicola says, »Yes, I think so.« Who is right?
S5: Colin.
 L: Yes. They haven't…
      Then Maria says, »I want to ring my parents. Does anybody know where the
      nearest phone box is?«
      Colin says, »I think there's one on the camp site.«
      Sue tells her, »No, it's in the village.« Who is right?
S6: Sue.
 L: Yes. It's in the village.

III Reproduzieren

Information erfragen und erteilen

Die Schüler arbeiten mit Partnern. Partner A bekommt Arbeitsblatt A, Partner B Blatt B.

Partner A	Partner B
It is your first day at a camp site in Britain and you need a lot of information. Ask your partner:	You have a summer job at a camp site in Britain. A lot of people ask you for information. Answer their questions.
1. Are there any... here? (shops/showers/cinemas/...)	1. – Yes,... (just round the corner/on the left/...). – There aren't any here. But there are some in town/...).
2. Have you any...? (information about.../stamps/ comics/...)	2. – Yes,... (here you are/how many?/...). – Sorry, I haven't anything at the moment. – You can't get any here, but try...
3. Do you know anything about...? (buses to.../train times/the cine-mas/library opening hours/...)	3. – Yes,... – Sorry, I don't know anything about that.
4. Can I get anything to... here? (eat/drink/read)	4. – Yes,... – You can't get anything on the camp site, but (there's a/try...).
5. Can I buy... anywhere round here?	5. – Yes,... – No, but...
6. Is there a... anywhere round here?	6. – Yes,... – No, but...
Now give this sheet to your partner and start again.	Now give this sheet to your partner and start again.

Geben Sie für jede Frage ein Modellgespräch vor. Im Klassenverband wird das jeweilige Gespräch dann kurz geübt, wobei der Wortschatz von den Schülern variiert werden kann.

L: Look at Partner A's sheet (lesen Sie vor): It's your first day at a camp site in Britain and you need a lot of information. Ask your partner, »Are there any shops here?« or »Are there any showers here?« Now look at Partner B's sheet: You have a summer job at a camp site in Britain. A lot of people ask you for information. Answer their questions. So let's answer Partner A's first question: »Are there any shops here?« – Partner B can say, »Yes, just round the corner« or »There aren't any here. But there are some in town«, or »in the village«. Who wants to try this conversation?

S1: Are there any washing machines here?

S2: Yes, on the left.

L: What about the second question on Partner A's sheet? You can ask, »Have you any information about this area?« or »Have you any stamps?« And Partner B can answer, »Yes, here you are« or »Sorry, I haven't anything at the moment« or »You can't get any here, but try the village« or »the shop down the road«. Who wants to try this conversation?

S3: Have you any comics?

S4: You can't get any here, but try the village.
    usw.

IV Produzieren

Information erfragen und erteilen
Die Gespräche werden in Partnerarbeit ohne Hilfe des Lehrers geübt. Anschließend können einzelne Paare ihre Gespräche vorführen.

V Bewußtmachung

We use **any, anything, anybody and anywhere**
1. for questions when we do not know the answer.
    Are there **any** shops here?
    Do you know **anything** about the buses?
    Does **anybody** know where the nearest phone box is?
    Can I buy stamps **anywhere** round here?
2. to give negative answers.
    There aren't **any** shops here.
    Sorry, I haven't **any** information at the moment.
    I don't know **anything** about that.
    I don't know **anybody** who can help you.
    There isn't a phone **anywhere** round here.

Comparison of adjectives: -er, -est

I Demonstration

Führen Sie die Komparativ- und Superlativformen der folgenden Adjektive durch Vergleiche zwischen vier verschiedenen Autos, die Sie an die Tafel bzw. auf den Tageslichtprojektor zeichnen, ein: *old/new, big/small, dirty/clean.* Die Autos sind jeweils von verschiedener Farbe, Größe und Sauberkeit und verschieden alt. Beispiel:

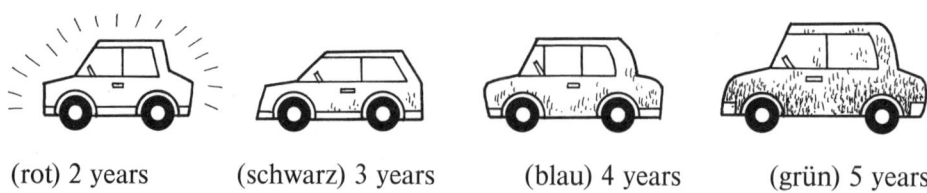

| (rot) 2 years | (schwarz) 3 years | (blau) 4 years | (grün) 5 years |

Tragen Sie die Grundform der Adjektive in die linke Spalte der folgenden Tabelle an der Tafel bzw. auf dem Tageslichtprojektor ein:

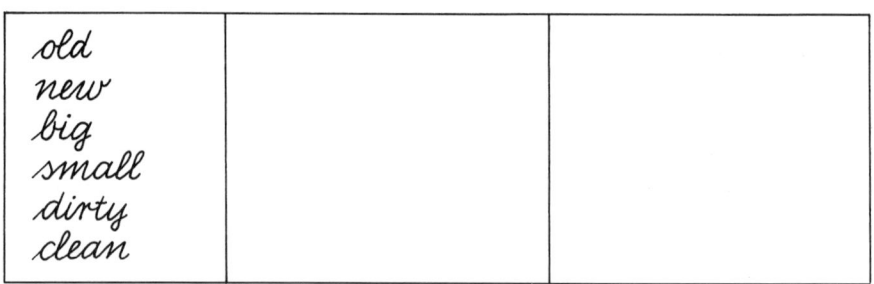

old new big small dirty clean		

Während Sie die Autos vergleichen, schreiben Sie die Komparativ- und Superlativformen der Adjektive in die Tabelle:

L: Look at the red car. It's two years <u>old.</u> The black car is <u>older than</u> the red one (car). The blue car is <u>older than</u> the black one. The green car is <u>the oldest.</u>
The blue car is quite <u>new,</u>...
The red car is not very <u>big,</u>...
usw.

Um weitere Adjektive einzuführen, skizzieren Sie vier Personen mit Namensangaben an die Tafel bzw. auf den Tageslichtprojektor. Sie gehören alle dem gleichen Geschlecht an, sind aber verschiedenen Alters und von unterschiedlicher Gestalt. Folgende Adjektive bieten sich an: *old/young, short/tall, thin/fat.*

Beispiel:

Vergleichen Sie die Personen in der gleichen Weise wie oben und tragen Sie die Adjektive in die Tabelle ein:

young	*younger than*	*the youngest*
...	...	...

L: Look at Tony. He's quite <u>young.</u> Johnny's <u>younger than</u> Tony. Alan's
<u>younger than</u> Johnny. Peter's <u>the youngest.</u>
Alan's quite <u>short.</u> Johnny's shorter than ...
Tony's not very <u>tall</u> ...
usw.

II Verstehen und Reagieren

Geheime Auswahl
Fordern Sie die Schüler abwechselnd auf, sich eines der abgebildeten Autos bzw. eine der Personen auszusuchen. Durch Fragen folgender Art versuchen Sie, die jeweilige Auswahl zu erraten:
    L: Is it a car (person)? Is it the biggest/bigger than the red one?
Die Lernenden antworten nur mit »yes« bzw. »no«.

III Reproduzieren

Information erfragen und geben
Die Lernenden benutzen die neuen Strukturen, um in Kettenfragen Informationen über ihre Mitschüler zu bekommen.

Comparative

tall/short: Mit Hilfe eines mitgebrachten Meterstabs mißt der Lehrer seine eigene
Größe (an der Wand):

    L: I'm (1,70 m) tall. (S1), are you taller or shorter than me?

    S1: (mißt sich) I'm (1,65 m). (S2), are you taller or shorter than me?

        usw.

old/young:

    L: I've got a sister. She's younger than me. What about you, (S1)?

    S1: I've got a sister, too/brother. (S)he's older/younger than me. What about
        you,…?

        I haven't any brothers or sisters. What about you,…?

Superlative

young:

    L: I'm the oldest person in the family. What about you, (S1)? Are you the
        youngest?

    S1: Yes. What about you, (S2)?

        No, my (sister)'s the youngest.

    S2: I'm/My (brother)'s the youngest. What about you,…?

        usw.

In der gleichen Weise können die Superlativformen von *tall/short* und *long/short*
geübt werden:

    L: I'm the tallest/shortest in the family. What about you, (S1)?

    S1: I'm the…/My (mother)'s the …est.

    L: I've got the longest/shortest hair in the family…

        usw.

IV Produzieren

Quiz

Stellen Sie Listen von Gegenständen, Tieren, Ortsnamen, Flüssen usw. mit zu
ihrer Beschreibung passenden Adjektiven zusammen. Sie können Information
über die Zielkultur einfließen lassen (1, 2) oder zusätzlich zur Grammatikübung
Vokabeln wiederholen (6, 7).

Beispiele:

1. Birmingham – London – Manchester (big/small)
2. Sears Tower (Chicago) – the Eiffel Tower – the Empire State building (high:
   Sears Tower is the highest: 548 m)
3. Alaska – Morocco – Great Britain (hot/cold)

4. Mississippi − Nile − Amazon (long: the Nile is the longest: 6670 km)
5. Antelope − horse − tiger (fast/slow)
6. Mineral water − coke − whisky (dear/cheap)
7. Eleven thirty-two, twenty-seven minutes to twelve, one minute after half past eleven (early/late).
usw.

Teilen Sie die Klasse in zwei Mannschaften, die sich mit Hilfe der Liste abwechselnd Fragen stellen und beantworten. Punkte können für inhaltlich korrekte Antworten und auch für sprachlich korrekte Fragen verteilt werden. Fragen und Antworten sind wie folgt zu formulieren:

Frage: Is (Sears Tower) (high)er than (the Eiffel Tower)?
         Which is the (fast)est: an antelope, a horse or a tiger?
Antwort: Yes, I think so/No, I don't think so/...

Geben Sie den Mannschaften genügend Zeit, ihre Fragen vorzubereiten. Ermutigen Sie die Lernenden dazu, eigene Beispiele für die Liste beizutragen. Die Lernenden werden dadurch stärker aktiviert und erweitern ihren Wortschatz, indem sie nach neuen Vokabeln fragen bzw. sie selbständig (auch in Hausarbeit) nachschlagen.

V Bewußtmachung

To make comparisons with <u>short</u> adjectives we add <u>-er than</u> or <u>the -est.</u>

   old − older than − the oldest

Bemerkung:
Im britischen Englisch werden einsilbige Adjektive zunehmend mit *more* und *most* gesteigert, z.B. *more cheap.*

Comparison of adjectives: more, most

I Demonstration

Legen Sie den folgenden Fragebogen auf den Tageslichtprojektor oder kopieren Sie ihn an die Tafel und erklären ihn wie folgt.

Questionnaire		
Name: *Sylvia Watson*		
More interesting?	yes	no
1. Football is more interesting than swimming.	☒	☐
2. Volleyball is more exciting than basketball.	☐	☒
3. Skiing is more difficult than skating.	☒	☐
The most dangerous?		
1. Boxing is the most dangerous sport.	☐	☒
2. Cricket is the most boring sport.	☒	☐
3. Tennis is the most popular sport in this country.	☐	☒

L: Yesterday a girl came up to me in the playground. She gave me a questionnaire like this one. Her class wants to find out what people think about sports. So they are giving people questionnaires. They gave this questionnaire to a girl called Sylvia Watson (man kann auch einen bekannten Namen einsetzen, z.B. den einer Lehrkraft).
Let's see what Sylvia thinks about sports, then. (Liest): »Football is more interesting than swimming.« — »Yes«. So she thinks football is more interesting than swimming, doesn't she? She says that volleyball isn't more exciting than basketball — she thinks basketball is more exciting. And she thinks skiing is more difficult than skating. That's interesting, isn't it?
Let's go on: Sylvia doesn't think that boxing is the most dangerous sport. She thinks cricket is the most boring sport and that tennis is the most popular sport in this country. Now I wonder if you all agree with Sylvia?

II Verstehen und Reagieren

Information geben
Stellen Sie den Schülern die aufgelisteten Fragen der Reihe nach vor. Stellen Sie die gleiche Frage an 4–5 Schüler. Die Schüler antworten mit »yes« bzw. »no«:

L: Let's see what you all think. (S1), is football more interesting than swimming?

S1: Yes (it is).

L: And you, (S2)? Is football more interesting than swimming?

S2: No (it isn't).

L: Ah, I see. What about you, (S3)? Is…?

usw.

III Reproduzieren

Alternativfragen: Auskunft erfragen und erteilen
Teilen Sie jedem Schüler folgenden Fragebogen aus. Je nach Wortschatz und Interessenlage können Sie die angegebenen Freizeitaktivitäten ändern. Fragen Sie die Klasse nach ihren Freizeitaktivitäten mit Hilfe des Fragebogens und des Dialogmusters. Lassen Sie dabei die Fragebogen von jedem Schüler ausfüllen:

Questionnaire

Name:....................................

More relaxing?   a/b/n
1. a) doing sports b) watching sport on TV – more relaxing?   ☐
2. a) watching TV b) going out with friends – more important?   ☐
3. a) learning a language b) learning to cook – more useful?   ☐
4. a) listening to pop music b) listening to folk songs – more exciting? ☐
5. a) reading a book b) watching the film of the book – more
   interesting?   ☐

The most interesting?
6. Football, swimming, volleyball, basketball, skiing, skating,
   boxing, cricket, tennis, ice-hockey…?

The most					
interesting	exciting	difficult	dangerous	boring	popular in this country

---

Dialogmuster

More relaxing?
> L: Is X more... than Y?
> Or is Y more... than X?
> S: X is more... (than Y).
> I'm not sure.
> Both are...
> Sometimes X is more... than Y.
> It depends. ...
> ...

Beispiel:
> L: (S1), is doing sports more relaxing than watching sports on TV? Or is watching sports on TV more relaxing than doing sports?
> S1: Watching sports on TV is more relaxing.

Ermuntern Sie fortgeschrittenere Schüler dazu, detailliertere Antworten zu geben, indem Sie nachfragen, z.B.: *It depends. Sometimes I find... more relaxing. For example, when I'm very tired. Sometimes I want to...* Die Lernenden können sich auch gegenseitig nach weiteren Auskünften befragen.

Die gleiche Frage wird mehreren Schülern gestellt, dann wird die jeweilige Antwort in den Fragebogen eingetragen:

> L: All right. Let's fill in our answers to this question now: if you think doing sports is more relaxing than watching sports on TV put »a« in the box. But if you find watching sports on TV more relaxing write »b«. If you're not sure write »n«.
> Now let's have a look at the next questions.

Auf diese Weise werden die Fragen 1–5 durchgearbeitet.

Frage 6:
Dialogmuster

The most interesting?
> L: Which is the most interesting, exciting, difficult, dangerous or boring sport?
> Which is the most popular sport in this country?
> S1: I think (football) is the most (boring).
> S2: I do, too./So do I.
> I don't. ... is the most (boring).
> ... is the most (exciting).
> Oh no, the most (exciting) is...

Beispiel:

L: Now let's see what you all think: Which is the most interesting sport? Which is the most exciting, the most difficult, the most dangerous or the most boring sport? Which is the most popular sport in this country? (S1), what do you think?

S1: I think (football) is the most (boring).

L: Do you? Well, what about the others? Is football the most boring sport?

S2: No, cricket's the most boring.

S3: Oh no, cricket's the most exciting.

S4: No, the most exciting is basketball.

usw.

Geben Sie nun den Schülern etwas Zeit, um Frage 6 auszufüllen.

IV Produzieren

Ergebnisse berichten

Die Ergebnisse werden zu einem Klassenprofil zusammengestellt. Sie können die Schüler bitten, Prognosen aufzustellen, indem jeder aufschreibt, welche Antwort wahrscheinlich am meisten Zustimmung finden wird, z.B.: 1b, 2b, 3a, 4a, 5a, 6 *interesting – football, exciting – ice-hockey* usw.

Dann werden die Fragebogen untereinander ausgetauscht. Die Antworten werden vorgelesen und von der Lehrkraft bzw. von einem Lernenden wie folgt an der Tafel bzw. auf dem Tageslichtprojektor zusammengetragen, z.B.:

1. a) 14   b) 12   n) 4
2. a) 10   b) 18   n) 2

usw.

6. The most interesting
football: (Strichliste) 1 1 1 1 1 1 1:   7
swimming: 1 1 1 1:   4

usw.

The most exciting
football: 1 1 1 1 1 1:   6
swimming: 1 1 1:   3

usw.

In großen Klassen sammeln Gruppen zunächst die Ergebnisse, und ein Gruppensprecher liest sie dann der Klasse vor. In diesem Fall schreibt der Gruppensprecher die Ergebnisse wie folgt auf und berichtet dann in der 3. Person:

1. a) 3   b) 2   n) 1

Gruppen-
sprecher: Three people think that doing sports is more relaxing than watching sports on TV; two think that watching sports on TV is more relaxing than doing sports; one isn't sure.

usw.

In kleineren Klassen liest jeder Schüler die ihm vorliegenden Antworten vor:

S: (Fragen 1-5): This is what Axel thinks: watching sports on TV is more relaxing than doing sports; going out with friends is more important than watching TV;...

(Frage 6): The most interesting sport is basketball, the most exciting is... usw.

Die Ergebnisse an der Tafel können mit den Prognosen verglichen werden: *Who wrote down »a« for number 1?* usw. In fortgeschritteneren Klassen können die Ergebnisse und Prognosen diskutiert werden.

Weitere Übungsmöglichkeiten

1. Der Fragebogen kann auch anderen Personen (Mitschülern anderer Klassen, Familienmitgliedern) vorgelegt werden. Die Ergebnisse werden dann in der nächsten Stunde vorgetragen.

2. In Gruppen- oder Partnerarbeit wird ein ähnlicher Fragebogen zu einem anderen Thema erstellt. Das Thema wird entweder von der Klasse oder der Lehrkraft vorgeschlagen, z.B. *What sort of books/films do most people like?* Wenn die Schüler die Fragen selbst erarbeiten, hat das den Vorteil, daß sie stärker motiviert sind, nach dem dafür notwendigen Wortschatz zu fragen bzw. zu suchen. Stichwörter können als Hilfestellung vorgeschlagen werden, z.B.:

- relaxing/interesting/exciting/boring/realistic/romantic/popular at the moment/ expensive/difficult/dangerous to make (films)
- western/love stories/thrillers/science fiction stories/war stories
- films about schoolchildren/gangsters/different countries
- watching films on TV/going to the cinema/theatre
- What was the most interesting/exciting... film/book you ever saw/read?

V Bewußtmachung

To make comparisons with <u>longer</u> adjectives (with two or more syllables) we use <u>more</u> and <u>most</u>.

       useful - more useful - the most useful

       interesting - ... - ...

Die Schüler können weitere Beispiele aus der vorausgegangenen Lektion in die Tabelle eintragen.

Bemerkung:

Im britischen Englisch werden ein- und zweisilbige Adjektive zunehmend mit *more* und *most* gesteigert, z.B. *more cheap, more clever, more easy.*

Future continuous

I Demonstration

Führen Sie das Thema ein, indem Sie über das kommende Wochenende sprechen. Dabei kann der Wortschatz auf der Folie schon vorweggenommen werden.

    L: Have you any plans for next weekend? (Geben Sie den Lernenden die Gelegenheit, kurz darauf zu antworten.)

         I'm going to have a great weekend. Just think – this time next Saturday I'll be (climbing a mountain/skiing/...).

Legen Sie die Folie auf den Tageslichtprojektor.

    L: Look at all these people. They're all waiting for a bus. Some of them are going on holiday next week. They're thinking of the great time they're going to have.

         Marie's thinking, »This time next week I'll be lying on a beach.«

         Paul's thinking, »This time next week I'll be skiing.«

         usw.

Weitere Bildbeschreibungen

Diane: climbing a mountain; Richard and Sarah: touring Italy; Carol: hiking in Scotland; Bob: sightseeing in Paris; Ann: camping in Ireland; Pete and Jane: hitch-hiking in Spain

II Verstehen und Reagieren

Gedächtnisspiel: Geheime Auswahl

Stellen Sie sich vor, Sie sind eine der abgebildeten Personen. Erzählen Sie bei abgedeckter Folie, was Sie in der nächsten Woche um diese Zeit machen werden. Die Schüler versuchen herauszufinden, an wen Sie denken.

L: Look at this picture for a few minutes and try to remember it. (Decken Sie das Bild nach einigen Minuten zu.)
Now let's see how good your memories are.
Listen: Next week at this time I'll be sightseeing in Paris. Who am I?

S1: Ann?

L: No. Who knows?

S2: Bob?

L: That's right. Now listen again: Next week at this time...
usw.

III Reproduzieren

Information erteilen

Mit Hilfe des Wortschatzes auf der Folie stellen sich die Lernenden einen schönen Urlaub vor, den sie nächste Woche antreten werden. Ermutigen Sie sie auch dazu, andere Tätigkeiten zu nennen und nach unbekanntem Wortschatz zu fragen bzw. zu suchen.

L: Imagine you're going on a wonderful holiday next week. Tell us about it. I'll start. Listen, I'll tell you about my dream holiday.
This time next week I'll be skiing in Switzerland. What about you (S1)?

S1: I'll be sightseeing in New York.

S2: I'll be sailing round the world.
usw.

IV Produzieren

Bildbeschreibung

Das Folienbild wird schriftlich beschrieben.

L: Now write about all these different people. Start like this: This time next week Marie will be ...ing. Paul will be ...ing.
usw.

V Bewußtmachung

We use the future continuous when we are dreaming about or imagining something that will be happening at a specific time in the future, e.g.

This time next week **I will be lying** on a beach.

Future: going to

A. Affirmative statements: She's/I'm going to
B. Negative statements: She's not going to

A. Affirmative statements

I Demonstration

Anhand der Bilder beschreiben Sie, was Caroline im Urlaub vorhat:
camera – take some photos
books – read some books/thrillers
bikini – go swimming
writing pad, envelopes – write some letters
train time-table – go/travel by train
Italian course – learn Italian
tennis racquet – play tennis
youth hostel guide – stay in a youth hostel
paint box – paint
book on museums – visit some museums

    L: (Deuten Sie auf die jeweiligen Einzelbilder und schreiben Sie während Ihres Vortrags einige Beispielsätze auf): Look, this is Caroline. Next week she wants to go on holiday. Let's see what her plans are. (Schreiben Sie das

Wort *plans* auf, um die Funktion von *going to* klarzustellen.) She's going to take some photos. She's going to read some books – some thrillers. She's going to go swimming... usw.

II Verstehen und Reagieren

Gedächtnisspiel: richtig oder falsch?
Geben Sie der Klasse einige Minuten Zeit, um sich die Bilder zu merken, und decken Sie die Bilder dann zu.

L: Now look at these pictures and try to remember them. But don't write anything down. (Die Bilder sind zugedeckt): Now can you remember Caroline's plans? Listen: She's going to read some thrillers. Is that right or wrong? Say »That's right« or »That's wrong«.

S1: That's right.

L: Yes, that's right. She's going to read some thrillers. Listen again: She's going to travel by plane. Is that right or wrong?

S2: That's wrong.

usw.

Weitere mögliche »Falschaussagen«: *She's going to write some postcards, learn French, read some comics, books about..., play table tennis, draw, visit some churches.*

III Reproduzieren

Gedächtnisspiel: Falsche Aussagen korrigieren
Decken Sie die Bilder kurz auf, dann wieder zu.

L: Now look at the pictures for a moment. (Bei zugedeckten Bildern): Listen again. But this time correct me: Caroline's going to travel by boat.

S1: No (that's wrong), she's going to travel by train.

L: Yes, that's right. She's going to travel by train, isn't she? Listen again: she's going to stay in a hotel.

usw.

IV Produzieren

Informationen geben
Um die Lernenden dazu zu befähigen, über ihre eigenen (realen oder fiktiven) Urlaubspläne zu berichten, geben Sie einige Wahlmöglichkeiten in Form von *multiple choice* Aussagen an. Der Wortschatz soll dem Alter und der Interessenlage der Lernenden angepaßt werden, z.B.:

L: Now think of your next holiday. Make some plans. Here are some ideas. Put a cross (×) in the right box or write down your own ideas. Later you can tell everybody what you're going to do.

Ermutigen Sie die Lernenden, nach unbekanntem Wortschatz zu fragen bzw. zu suchen.

Arbeitsblatt

My holiday plans

I am going to have a holiday
☐ next week
☐ in summer   and I am
☐ ....

going to stay
☐ in the USA.
☐ at home.   I am going to travel
☐ ....

☐ by bike.
☐ by train.   I am going to spend my holiday
☐ ....
☐ alone
☐ with a friend
☐ ....

and I am/we are going to stay
☐ in a youth hostel.
☐ with friends.
☐ ....

I am/We are going to
☐ stay in one place all the time.
☐ travel around.
☐ visit.........
☐ ....

I am going to
☐ read.
☐ take photos, too.
☐ ....

I usually write
☐ about 3
☐ between 3 and 10   postcards when I am on
☐ ....

holiday.   I know I am going to write one to
☐ my mother
☐ my neighbour
☐ ....

this time.

Die Schüler tragen ihre Pläne entweder der Klasse, einer Gruppe oder einem Partner vor *(I'm going to... What about you?).*

B. Negative statements

Um die Verneinung einzuführen, ändern Sie die Lektion etwas. Fügen Sie einigen Bildern, die wie oben Carolines Pläne darstellen, weitere Bilder, Wörter oder Ausdrücke hinzu. Sie sind durchgestrichen, um zu zeigen, daß Caroline nicht die Absicht hat, diesen Tätigkeiten nachzugehen, z.B.:

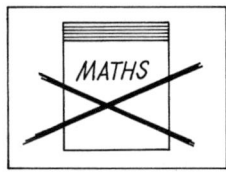 *She's not going to do maths.*

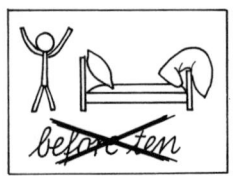 *She's not going to get up before ten.*

Erklären Sie den Schülern während des Demonstrationsvortrags die Bedeutung dieser Symbole. Ansonsten verläuft die Lektion wie unter A.

V Bewußtmachung

We use <u>going to</u> for things we <u>plan</u> to do.
>   Caroline is **going to** take photos on holiday.
>   She is not **going to** get up before ten.

Future with present continuous

6 MON	play table-tennis, 8.00	**10** FRI	7.30 baby-sit
7 TUES	6.00 practise with orchestra	**11** SAT	10.00 go shopping with Mum 8.00 sing with band
8 WED	7.00 meet John in town		
9 THURS	7.30 circus	**12** SUN	12.00 lunch at Angela's

I Demonstration

Die Tagebucheinträge werden dem jeweiligen Alter und der Interessenlage der Lernenden angepaßt. Wählen Sie dabei Tätigkeiten aus, die für einen bestimmten Zeitpunkt ausgemacht wurden (nicht z.B. *clean the windows*).
Führen Sie das Thema *diary* ein.

L: Do any of you keep a diary? Do you write a lot in it? Do you just write down the things you have to do or do you write other things as well?

Geben Sie den Lernenden die Gelegenheit, kurz darauf zu antworten. Beschreiben Sie dann die obigen Tagebucheinträge und schreiben Sie dabei Ihre Sätze auf.

L: Look at this diary (Tafel oder Tageslichtprojektor). It belongs to a girl called Diana. She's always very busy in the evenings. Let's see what she's doing next week.
Next Monday she's playing table tennis.
On Tuesday she's practising with the orchestra.
On Wednesday she's meeting John in town.
On Thursday she's going to the circus.
On Friday she's baby-sitting.
On Saturday morning she's going shopping with her mother.
On Saturday evening she's singing with a band.
And on Sunday she's having lunch at Angela's.

II Verstehen und Reagieren

1. Information erfragen und erteilen
Lesen Sie die einzelnen Eintragungen vor, ohne den jeweiligen Tag zu nennen. Er soll von den Schülern herausgefunden werden.

L: Diana's going to be very busy next week, isn't she? Let's see. She's baby-sitting one evening. When's that?

S1: On Friday.

L: And one day she's playing table tennis.

S2: On Monday.
usw.

2. Falschaussagen
Ohne auf die Folie zu schauen, wiederholen Sie die Eintragungen, wobei Sie bewußt einige inhaltliche Fehler machen.

L: So she's baby-sitting on Monday. Is that right?

S1: No, on Friday.

L: Oh yes, of course. She's baby-sitting on Friday. And she's going to the circus on Thursday. That's right, isn't it?

S2: Yes.

L: She's having lunch at Angela's on Saturday.

S3: No, on Sunday.
usw.

III Reproduzieren

Information erfragen und erteilen
Geben Sie Auskunft über die festen Vereinbarungen, die Sie für die nächste Zeit (*tonight, on Saturday, at the weekend, at Easter*…) getroffen haben, und fragen Sie die Schüler nach ihren Plänen.

L: I'm going to the theatre tonight. I've already bought my ticket. What about you? Are you doing anything tonight? (Ermutigen Sie die Lernenden, nach unbekanntem Wortschatz zu fragen bzw. zu suchen; neuer Wortschatz wird angeschrieben.)

S1: I'm watching videos with a friend tonight.

S2: I'm …/not doing anything.
usw.

L: What about the weekend? Are you doing anything? I'm (playing volleyball/ …) on Saturday afternoon.

S1: I'm…
usw.

IV Produzieren

Vereinbarungen treffen
Teilen Sie folgendes Arbeitsblatt aus.

6 MON	_____	10 FRI	_____
7 TUES	_____	11 SAT	_____
8 WED	_____		
9 THURS	_____	12 SUN	_____

Die Lernenden machen zuerst auf dem Arbeitsblatt ihre persönlichen Einträge für die Woche mit Zeitangaben. Dann versuchen sie, miteinander Vereinbarungen zu treffen. Jedes Blatt wird andere Eintragungen aufweisen.

L: What are you doing next week? Write down four things on four different days. (S1), you might be doing something on Wednesday, Friday, Saturday and Sunday. (S2), you might be doing something on Monday, Tuesday, Friday and Saturday. So all your diaries will be different.

In Einzel- oder Partnerarbeit werden die Einträge gemacht. Dabei dienen die Stichworte auf der Folie und der zusätzliche Wortschatz, den Sie während der Phase III aufgeschrieben haben, als Muster.

Bevor Sie folgendes Gespräch beginnen, schreiben Sie die dazu notwendigen Strukturen als Hilfestellung auf:

Are you doing anything on/next...?

Yes, I'm ...ing.
No. Why?

L: (S1), are you doing anything on Wednesday?
S1: No. Why?
L: I'm (going to the cinema). Do you want to come?
S1: Yes, great/No, not really.
L: Now you (S1) ask someone, »Are you doing anything next Monday or next Saturday morning or on Friday night?«
S1: (S2), are you doing anything on Tuesday evening?
S2: Yes, I'm playing table tennis.
L: Now you (S3) ask someone.
S3: (S4), are you doing anything on Saturday afternoon?
S4: No. Why?
S3: Because I'm going swimming. Do you want to come?

V Bewußtmachung

We use the present continuous for something that we have <u>arranged</u> (»verein-
baren«) for some time in the future. We often give the time or date.
What **are** you **doing** tomorrow night?
I**'m going** to the cinema with Jill. She's already bought the tickets.
I**'m meeting** Tony on Saturday. I promised to go swimming with him.

Future perfect

I Demonstration

Legen Sie die Liste 1 auf den Tageslichtprojektor oder schreiben Sie sie an die Tafel.

Liste 1:

- pay milkman
- change money
- fetch tickets
- give key to Mrs Kent
- take dog to neighbours'
- water plants
- order taxi to station

Erklären Sie die Liste folgendermaßen:

L: Frank is going on holiday on Saturday afternoon. Before he leaves, though, he has a lot of things to do. He's written everything down: He has to pay the milkman, change money... usw.

Zeigen Sie nun die Tabelle:

	MON	TUES	WED	THURS	FRI	SAT
pay milkman						
change money						
fetch tickets						
give key to Mrs Kent						
take dog to neighbours'						
water plants						
order taxi to station						

L: Frank looks at the list and says, »There are so many things to do. I hope I'll have done them all by Saturday. Let me see: I'll have paid the milkman by Monday, I'll have changed money by...«
usw.

Tragen Sie nach jeder solchen Aussage einen Haken in die entsprechende Spalte ein, z.B. bei der ersten Aussage neben *pay the milkman* und unter *MON*:

    change money – Thurs.

    fetch tickets – Wed.

    give key to Mrs Kent – Tues.

    take dog to neighbours' – Sat.

    water plants –Fri.

    order taxi – Wed.

L: So now Frank thinks that by Saturday he'll have done everything. But that's what he thinks! You see, I've just found a second list. I think he's forgotten all about this one. Let's see what it says:

Liste 2:

```
- take library books back
- collect anorak from cleaner's
- pay bills
- stop post
- answer Steve's letter
- give holiday address to Sue
```

L: So he won't have done everything, will he? Let's see: He won't have taken his library books back, he won't have… usw.

II Verstehen und Reagieren

Anweisungen befolgen: Hören und schreiben

Teilen Sie ähnliche Tabellen aus, in denen jedoch nur die Wochentage eingetragen sind. Die noch ausstehenden Verpflichtungen werden später von den Lernenden eingesetzt. Die Lernenden machen nach Ihren Anweisungen ähnliche Einträge wie bei Ihrer Demonstration.

L: Frank isn't going on holiday alone. He's going with his friend, Tony. Tony has a lot to do, as well, before he can leave on Saturday. Let's help him to make a list and to write down when he's going to do everything.

Demonstrieren Sie die Arbeitsweise, indem Sie den ersten Eintrag in Ihrer eigenen, leeren Tabelle an der Tafel bzw. auf dem Tageslichtprojektor vornehmen. Benutzen Sie die gleichen Verben wie in Ihrem Demonstrationsgespräch, variieren Sie aber Wochentage, Verpflichtungen und Reihenfolge, z.B.:

L: He'll have fetched his tickets by Tuesday. So we'll write »fetch tickets« and put a tick under Tuesday.

	MON	TUES	WED	THURS	FRI	SAT
fetch tickets		✔				
...						

L: He'll have | paid the milkman by Wednesday.
taken the cat to his friend's by Friday.
changed money by Monday.
watered his plants by Saturday.
ordered a taxi by Thursday.
given his key to his neighbour by Friday.

L: (Nachdem die Einträge von den Schülern gemacht worden sind.) But there are still an awful lot of things to do. Tony knows he won't have time for them all before he goes on holiday on Saturday. So he's going to make a second list of things he has to do when he gets back from his holiday. Let's help him to write this list.

Demonstrieren Sie die Arbeitsweise an der Tafel bzw. am Tageslichtprojektor.

L: He won't have answered Jill's letter by Saturday. So we'll write »answer Jill's letter« so that he won't forget to do it when he gets back:

AFTER THE HOLIDAYS
– *answer Jill's letter*

Die Lernenden stellen nun die Liste nach Ihren Anweisungen zusammen:

L: He won't have | taken his library books back by Saturday.
collected his coat from the cleaner's.
paid his electricity bill.
cleaned his bike.
painted his garage door.

III Reproduzieren

Vorbereitungen treffen

Prüfen Sie die Richtigkeit der Antworten, indem Sie die Lernenden ihre Antworten vorlesen lassen und diese in Ihre eigene Tabelle eintragen:

L: Now let's see if you did it right. Tell me what Tony has to do before he can go on holiday on Saturday. He has to fetch tickets. He'll have fetched them by Tuesday, won't he? What else?

S1: He'll have paid the milkman by Wednesday. (Tragen Sie »pay milkman« und den Haken ein.)

S2: He'll have...

usw.

L: And what about the things he won't have done before Saturday? He won't have answered Jill's letter. And...?

S1: He won't have taken his library books back.

S2: He won't have...

usw.

IV Produzieren

Vorbereitungen treffen

Die Lernenden treffen Vorbereitungen für eine Party. Verschiedene Aufgaben werden an verschiedene Schüler verteilt, die dann planen, bis wann diese Aufgaben zu erledigen sind.

L: We often have to plan things, too, like Frank and Tony. For example, if you want to have a really good party there are lots of things you have to plan. You have to...?

Sammeln Sie Vorschläge. Ermutigen Sie die Lernenden dazu, nach unbekanntem Wortschatz zu fragen bzw. zu suchen:

write list of guests/write invitations/send the invitations out/buy, make (food, drink)/borrow some records, plates, glasses, barbeque grill... usw.

In Gruppen stellen die Lernenden einen Terminplan auf:

L: Let's make our plans. Let's say that (Bärbel) has to write all the invitations. She'll have written them by Thursday.

(Tafelanschrieb): write invitations — Bärbel, Thursday.

Get together in groups of four or five and plan your party like this.

Nach einiger Zeit referieren die Gruppen über ihre Pläne. Damit alle zu Wort kommen, trägt jeder einen Satz vor:

Gruppe 1: S1: Georg will have written the invitations by Monday.

S2: Karin will have sent them out by Tuesday.

usw.

V Bewußtmachung

We use the future perfect to say that something will or will not have been done by a certain time in the future.

Mike **will have changed** money **by Thursday.**

He **won't have answered** Steve's letter **by Saturday.**

Future: will/will not

Coffee more expensive	**Bus fares not to go up**	**The end of a cigarette factory**
Shops open on Sundays? – No!	**Americans on Saturn in 2000**	**No rain tomorrow**
Start of school holidays earlier	**More women with top jobs from 1995**	

I Demonstration

Erklären Sie diese Schlagzeilen wie folgt. Wenn Sie die Sätze mit *will* schon zu diesem Zeitpunkt anschreiben wollen, verwenden Sie die Langform (*will* und *will not* und nicht *'ll* und *won't*).

L: Look at these newspaper headlines. Can you understand them all? »Coffee more expensive« – that's easy, isn't it? Coffee will be more expensive. It will cost more. What about the next one? »Bus fares not to go up« – Bus fares won't go up. They won't cost more. That's good. (Erklären Sie, daß *will not* als *won't* ausgesprochen wird.)
usw.

Weitere Erklärungen:
The end of... – A cigarette factory will close.
Shops open... – The shops will not open on Sundays.
Americans... – The Americans will land on Saturn in 2000.
No rain... – It will not rain tomorrow.
Start of... – The school holidays will start earlier.
More women... – More women will have top jobs from 1995 / There will be more women with top jobs from 1995.

II Verstehen und Reagieren

Hörverstehen: Zuordnen
Geben Sie für jede Schlagzeile eine Erklärung, die das *will*-Futur enthält. Die Lernenden versuchen, die jeweils passende Schlagzeile herauszufinden.

L: Let's see if you've really understood these headlines. Listen. Which headline is this: Something will not cost more.

S1: »Bus fares not to go up«.
L: That's right. Now listen again.
   usw.

Vorschläge für weitere Erklärungen:
Coffee... – This will cost more soon.
The end... – Some people will lose their jobs.
Shops open... – We will not be able to buy things on this day.
Americans... – This will happen in about (9) years.
No rain... – Something will not happen tomorrow.
Start of... – These will change/be different.
More women... – Soon the bosses will not only be men.

III Reproduzieren

Falschaussagen
Geben Sie absichtlich falsche Interpretationen für einige der Schlagzeilen. Sie können z.B. die Aussagen in ihr Gegenteil verkehren oder Teile der Aussage verändern, z.B.:

Coffee more expensive – Coffee will <u>not</u> cost more.
The end of a cigarette factory – A cigarette factory will <u>open</u>.

L: Listen again. Is this right: The Americans will land on Mars in 2000?
S1: No. They'll land on Saturn.
L: That's right. They'll land on Saturn in 2000. (Wiederholen Sie jedesmal die richtige Antwort.)
   Now what about this? Listen: A cigarette factory will open.
S2: No. It will close.
L: That's right. A cigarette factory will close.
   usw.

Weitere »Falschaussagen«:
Bus fares – Bus fares <u>will</u> go up.
The end... – A cigarette factory will <u>open</u>/A <u>chocolate</u> factory will close.
Shops open... – The shops <u>will</u> open on Sundays.
No rain... – It <u>will</u> rain tomorrow.
Start of... – School holidays will <u>not</u> start earlier.
More women... – There will be more women with <u>no</u> jobs from 1995/with top jobs from <u>1998</u>.

Je nach Leistungsstand der Klasse kann diese Übung schwieriger gestaltet werden: die Schlagzeilen werden zugedeckt, und Ihre »Falschaussagen« müssen aus dem Gedächtnis heraus korrigiert werden. Diese Aktivität kann auch als Mannschaftswettbewerb organisiert werden.

IV Produzieren

Schlagzeilen interpretieren
In Partnerarbeit werden ähnliche Schlagzeilen ohne Ihre Hilfe interpretiert.
Einige Vorschläge:
Winters warmer in future, Sunny tomorrow, Coke more expensive, New disco not to open before May, More girls with »boys« jobs by 1995, The end of the youth club? No!, Princess Di to visit Germany next year.
Es ist hilfreich, folgende Strukturen anzuschreiben:

> It/There/... will be...
> Coke will cost...
> ... will not...

Lösungen:
Winters will be warmer in future.
It will be sunny tomorrow.
Coke will cost more.
The new disco will not open before May.
There will be more girls with »boys« jobs by 1995/More girls will have »boys« jobs by 1995.
The youth club will not close.
Princess Di will visit Germany next year.

V Bewußtmachung

For things that will happen sometime in the future, <u>whether we want them to or not,</u> we use

will (not) ... + infinitive

Coffee	**will**	**cost**	more.
It	**will not**	**rain**	tomorrow.
There	**will**	**be**	more women with top jobs.

If clauses I
Subclause: simple present – main clause: will/won't

I Demonstration

Führen Sie das Thema »Safari Park« wie folgt ein:

    L: Last weekend I went to a safari park. Do you know what that is?
    (Die Lernenden machen einige Erklärungsversuche.)
    L: You have to be very careful when you go into a safari park. You can't just walk about where you like, can you? You might meet a tiger! There are notices to tell you what to do and what not to do.

Erklären Sie folgende Verhaltensregeln im Safaripark. Kopieren Sie die Schilder an die Tafel bzw. auf den Tageslichtprojektor.

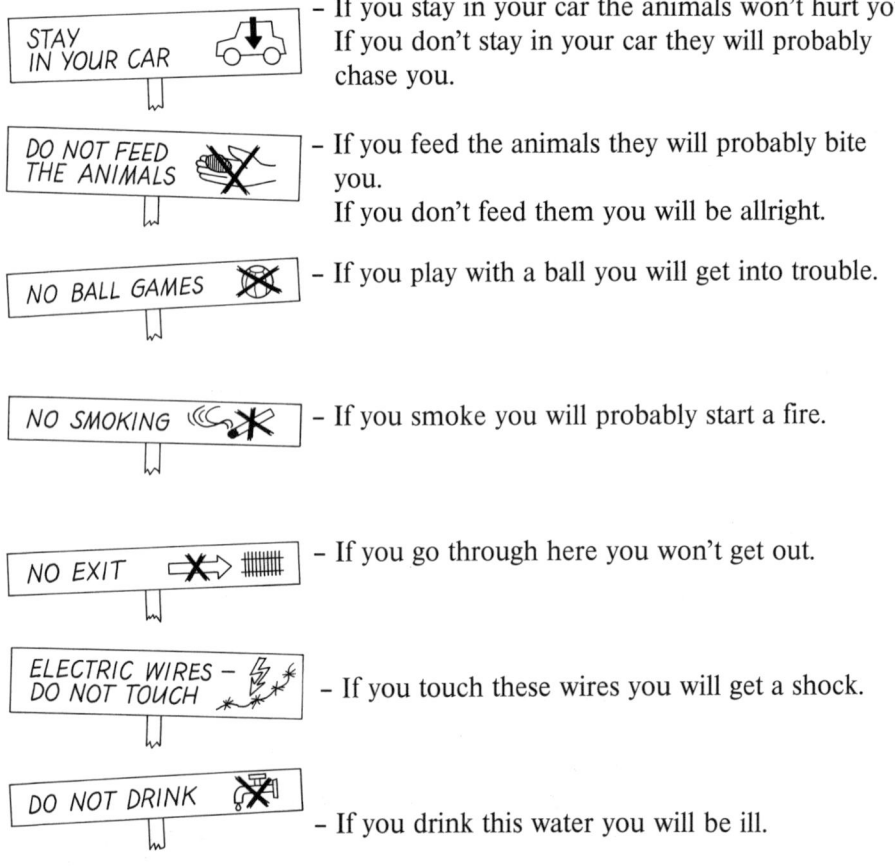

STAY IN YOUR CAR

– If you stay in your car the animals won't hurt you. If you don't stay in your car they will probably chase you.

DO NOT FEED THE ANIMALS

– If you feed the animals they will probably bite you.
If you don't feed them you will be allright.

NO BALL GAMES

– If you play with a ball you will get into trouble.

NO SMOKING

– If you smoke you will probably start a fire.

NO EXIT

– If you go through here you won't get out.

ELECTRIC WIRES – DO NOT TOUCH

– If you touch these wires you will get a shock.

DO NOT DRINK

– If you drink this water you will be ill.

L: »Stay in your car« – That means if you stay in your car the animals won't hurt you. If you don't stay in your car they'll probably chase you. »Do not feed the animals« – If you feed...
usw.

II Verstehen und Reagieren

Zuordnen
Zeigen Sie die folgenden weiteren Schilder.

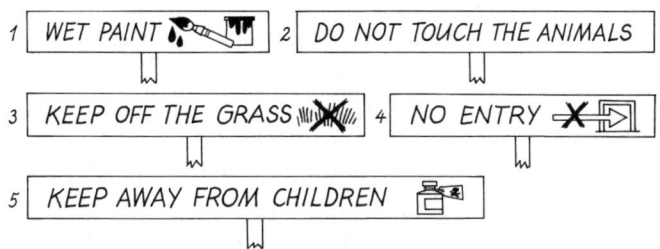

Die Lernenden versuchen nun, in Partnerarbeit Ihre Regelerklärungen den Schildern zuzuordnen. Halten Sie die Erklärungen vage, damit die Antworten nicht allzu offensichtlich sind:

L: Here are some more notices. I'm going to talk about them, but I'm not going to tell you which one I'm talking about. Listen and write down the number of the notice you think I'm talking about:
   – If you don't touch them they won't hurt you. (2)
   – If you don't do this you'll get into trouble. (3)
   – If you don't touch it you won't get dirty. (1)
   – If they drink this they'll be ill. (5)
   – If you do this you'll get into trouble. (4)

Prüfen Sie nun die Antworten nach:

L: If you don't touch them they won't hurt you. Which notice is that?

III Reproduzieren

Prognosen aufstellen
Die Schüler erwägen die Vor- und Nachteile eines Umzugs.

Manageress

for small town supermarket
in the North of Scotland

Good pay, travel, beautiful scenery.

L: Look at this notice. It's a different kind from those in the safari park isn't it? It's an advertisement for a job. A friend of mine, Mrs Hartnell, saw this advert in the paper and went for an interview. She got the job, but now she doesn't know if it's the right job for her or not.

She lives with her husband and two children in a small flat in London. She likes the job she has now, but she doesn't like London. She has always wanted to travel. And in the new job the pay is very good – more than both she and her husband get together now. So last night the family sat down and thought about it very carefully.

Carol – she's fourteen – wants to move. She says if they go to live in the country she'll learn to ride a horse. She can't do that in London. And they'll get a dog, too. Their London flat is too small for animals.

Dave's not sure. He's nineteen and he's just started work.

They decided to write all the positive and negative things down.

Zeigen Sie nun die folgende Liste.

	POSITIVE	NEGATIVE
Mum	– will get more money – will be able to travel	– will have to move
Dad	– won't have to work – will be able to stay at home	– will have to find another job
Carol	– will learn to ride a horse	– will have to change schools
Dave		– won't see his girlfriend any more – will have to change jobs
Everybody	– it will be quieter – will go for lots of walks – will get a dog	– won't see friends any more – won't visit family much – won't be as much to do

Anhand der Liste und des folgenden Dialogmusters wiegen die Lernenden die Vor- und Nachteile eines Umzugs gegeneinander ab.

Dialogmuster:

If...	(doesn't) (don't)	take(s) the job move (to the country) leave(s) London go(es) to Scotland/a small town go and live in Scotland/ the country	she they it there …	will won't	(have to) (be able to) …

   L: If Mrs Hartnell takes the job she'll get more money. That's good, isn't it? Is there anything else that's good about it for her?

Arbeiten Sie nun die Liste durch. Steuern Sie dabei die Schüleraussagen, indem Sie auf die relevanten Teile des Dialogmusters und der Liste deuten. Ermutigen Sie die Lernenden dazu, die Verben zu variieren, z.B.:

  S1:   If she takes the job she'll be able to travel.
   L: Now think of the negative things. If she takes the job...?
  S2:   They'll have to move.
   L: And if they move? What about Dad?
  S3:   If they move Dad will have to find another job.
   L: So if Mrs Hartnell takes the job her husband will have to change his job?
  S4:   No. He won't have to work. She'll get more money, so he'll be able to stay at home.
   L: If they go and live in Scotland Carol will be happy, won't she?
  S5:   Yes. If they move to the country she'll learn to ride a horse.
   L: And what about school?
  S6:   If they go to Scotland she'll have to change schools.
   L: If they don't move Dave will be happy, won't he?
  S7:   Yes. If his mother doesn't take the job he will be able to see his girlfriend.
  S8:   If they don't move he won't have to change jobs.
  S9:   If they go and live in Scotland they won't see their friends any more.
S10:   If they leave London they won't visit their family much.
   L: If they move it will be very different from London, won't it?
S11:   If they go and live in the country it will be quieter.
S12:   But if they go to a small town there won't be as much to do.
   L: But they'll enjoy some things, won't they?
S13:   If they move to the country they'll go for lots of walks.
S14:   And they'll get a dog.

IV Produzieren

Rollenspiel
Die Lernenden diskutieren nun die Vor- und Nachteile des Umzugs ohne Steuerung durch die Lehrkraft. Gruppenmitglieder übernehmen die Rollen der Eltern und der zwei Jugendlichen.

   L: Now let's imagine you're in this family. Talk about all these positive and negative things and then try to decide if you want to move or not. Maybe you can think of some more positive and negative things? Mrs Hartnell starts – like this:
Mrs Hartnell: »If I take the job we'll have much more money.«

Use as many of these beginnings (Tafel bzw. Tageslichtprojektor) as you can:

– If… take(s) the job…	– If… doesn't, don't take the job…
– If we move…	– If we don't move, stay here…
– If… leave(s) London…	– If… doesn't, don't leave London…
– If we go to Scotland/ a small town…	– If we don't go…
– If we go and live in the country/in Scotland…	

Anschließend führen die Gruppen ihre Gespräche vor und teilen der Klasse ihre Entscheidung mit: *We're (not) going to move/We don't know yet/…*

V Bewußtmachung

For things that <u>probably will or will not</u> happen under certain <u>conditions</u> we use

If + simple present for the conditions +   **will/won't**

If you **feed** the animals	they **will** bite you.
If Mrs Hartnell **doesn't take** the job	she **won't** have to move.

If clauses II
Subclause: simple past – main clause: would/could

I Demonstration

Mit Hilfe von einfachen Strichzeichnungen an der Tafel bzw. auf dem Tageslicht-projektor verdeutlichen Sie die folgenden Problemsituationen. Schreiben Sie da-bei die Beispielsätze (*If*-Sätze) an und unterstreichen Sie die Verben.

L: Today we're going to get to know some people who have problems. Alan's problem is that he's always tired.
If he <u>went</u> to bed earlier he <u>wouldn't be</u> so tired.

L: Now what about Ken and Linda? They have a big problem, haven't they?
If Linda <u>didn't go</u> to so many evening classes they <u>could go</u> out together.
And if Ken <u>didn't watch</u> TV every night they <u>would have</u> more time.

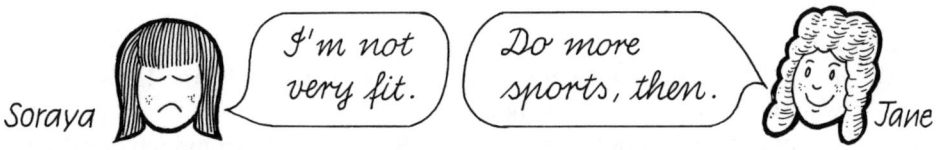

L: Soraya says she's not very fit.
If she <u>did</u> more sports she <u>would be</u> fitter.

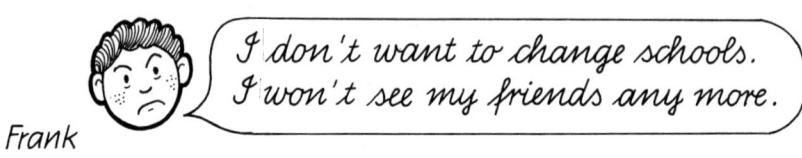

Frank

L: If Frank <u>changed</u> schools he <u>wouldn't see</u> his friends any more.

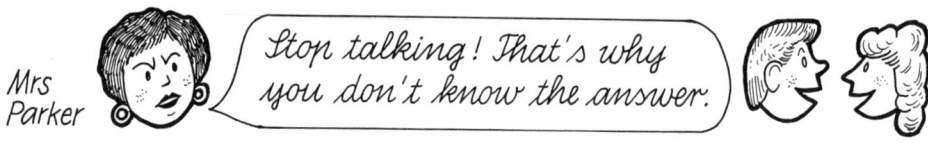

Mrs Parker

L: If they <u>didn't talk</u> so much they <u>would know</u> the answer.

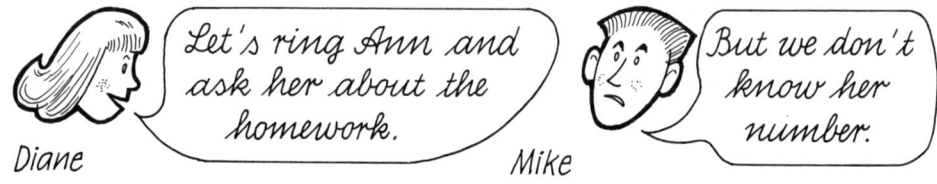

Diane   Mike

L: If they <u>knew</u> Ann's number they <u>could ring</u> her.

II Verstehen und Reagieren

Auskunft erteilen: Fragebogen
Die Lernenden füllen einen Fragebogen aus. Die Fragen sollten dem Alter der Lernenden angepaßt sein.

L: What would you do if you had a personal problem? Would you talk to a friend, a parent, a brother or sister? Or would you write to a magazine for help?

S1: I'd…

S2: I'd…

L: I've got a questionnaire here. It's all about personal problems. Let's find out what we'd do in difficult situations.

Teilen Sie nun die Fragebogen aus. Arbeiten Sie die Fragen mündlich durch und lassen Sie die Lernenden dabei den Fragebogen ausfüllen. Füllen Sie selbst auch einen Fragebogen aus.

Questionnaire

I **What would you do if...**   Mark your answers with ×.

1) you felt lonely one evening?
   ☐ I would watch TV or read a book.
   ☐ I would invite someone to come over.
   ☐ I would go out alone.

2) your friend said she/he didn't want to see you any more?
   ☐ I would go home and cry.
   ☐ I would look for another friend.
   ☐ I would try to talk to her/him about it.

3) someone asked you a personal question which you didn't want to answer?
   ☐ I would be angry.
   ☐ I would start talking about something else.
   ☐ I would tell her/him it was too personal.

4) someone criticised you?
   ☐ I would be angry and probably wouldn't talk to her/him for a few days.
   ☐ I would say she/he was wrong.
   ☐ I would ask for more details.

5) you thought people were talking about you?
   ☐ It wouldn't worry me. I would forget it.
   ☐ I would be unhappy, but I wouldn't say anything.
   ☐ I would ask someone about it.

Fragen Sie nun nach den Ergebnissen.
 L: Now let's see what you've all written down. What would you do if you felt
      lonely one evening?
 S1: (Liest die angekreuzte Antwort vor) I'd...
 S2: I'd...
      usw.

III Reproduzieren

Auskunft über sich selbst erteilen
Die Lernenden werden dazu ermutigt, sich zu überlegen, inwieweit ihr Leben anders wäre, wenn sich die Umstände änderten:

69

L: Let's think of different situations now. Not problems, but nice situations. What would we all do, for example, if we didn't have to go to school/work? Or if we could do exactly as we liked for a week?

Schreiben Sie nun paarweise If-Sätze auf, bei denen jedes Paar die gleiche Struktur aufweist. Nachdem Sie jeweils den ersten Satz vervollständigt haben, geben Sie mehreren Schülern die Gelegenheit, den zweiten Satz zu vollenden, z.B.:

1. If I didn't have to work I'd (travel all over the world/...)
2. If I didn't have to go to school I'd/I wouldn't...

3. If I could live where I liked...
4. If I could do what I liked for a week I'd/I wouldn't...

5. If I were a famous singer/painter/...
6. If I were a boy/girl/man/woman...

7. If I had a plane...
8. If I had lots of money...

Sie können die Übung verlängern, indem Sie nun umgekehrt vorgehen: Vollenden Sie den jeweils zweiten Satz in jedem Paar und lassen Sie die Lernenden den ersten vervollständigen.

IV Produzieren

Auskunft erteilen und erfragen
In Anlehnung an den Fragebogen stellen Gruppen jeweils eine Liste von ähnlichen Fragen zum Thema »What would you do in these situations?« zusammen. Geben Sie die unterstrichenen Strukturen vor und sammeln Sie einige Vorschläge für die Fragen, z.B.:
What would you do if...
1) your friend said or did something you didn't like?
2) your friend wanted to borrow your...?
3) the person sitting next to you on the bus started to cry?
4) ...

Nachdem die Fragen ausgearbeitet und von Ihnen auf ihre Richtigkeit hin überprüft worden sind, stellt jeweils ein Gruppenmitglied den Mitschülern eine der Fragen, die von seiner Gruppe zusammengestellt wurden. Die Antworten können auch diskutiert werden.
Der Lehrer kann auch selbst einige Vorschläge machen, z.B.: I wouldn't say anything/wouldn't talk to her/him for a few days/would tell other people about it/

wouldn't mind/would(n't) be very happy/would pretend not to see/would talk to her/him...

V Bewußtmachung

To talk about <u>conditions</u> that probably <u>will not or cannot</u> be fulfilled (a) or for <u>imaginary</u> situations (b) we use

If + simple past for the conditions +	**would/could**
a) **If** Diane and Mike **knew** Ann's number	they **could** ring her.
b) **If I felt** lonely	I **would** read a book.

71

If clauses III
Subclause: past perfect – main clause: would/might have/be

I Demonstration

Die Struktur wird anhand von Leserbriefen in einer Jugendzeitschrift eingeführt. Schreiben Sie die Briefe und Antwortschreiben an die Tafel bzw. auf den Tageslichtprojektor.

L: How many of you read teenage magazines? In some of them there are problem pages. They are pages where the readers can write about their problems and ask the magazine to help them. This is a problem page from a teenage magazine. The readers write to someone called Pete and he writes back to them.

Here's a letter from Sue Donnely. She says, »I took some of my records … do?« (Lesen Sie den Brief und die Antwort vor): And what does Pete say? »Nothing…« Well, I suppose he's right, isn't he? (Schreiben Sie den *if*-Satz an.)

*Lesen Sie nun alle Briefe und Antworten vor und unterstreichen Sie die **if**-Sätze.*

Dear Pete,
I took some of my records to the club last week and a boy stole them. What can I do?
                    Sue Donnely

Dear Sue,
Nothing now. But if you had written your name on them nobody would have stolen them, would they?

Dear Pete,
A friend asked me to go camping with her for a week. I quite like her, but a week is too long. Now she won't speak to me. What shall I do?
                    Jean Wilson

Dear Jean,
Explain that if you had gone away together you might both have been unhappy. But try it for just a weekend sometime.

Dear Pete,
I'm very unhappy at school. I wanted to leave last year but my teacher said I should stay and take the final exams in two years. What do you think?
                    Don Pearson

Dear Don,
Those exams will give you a better chance of getting the job you want. If you had left last year you might be very sorry now.

Dear Pete,
I asked my friend to lend me his bike. He wouldn't because he once lent me his library book and I spilled tea on it. Does this mean he will never lend me anything again?
                    Tony Wood

Dear Tony,
Well, you wouldn't have this problem if you hadn't been so careless, would you? He might change his mind one day.

Dear Pete,
There's a girl who lives in our street. I've always been afraid to talk to her, but yesterday I rang her and asked her out. Sie said yes, but now I don't know if it was right to ring her.

Chris Bennett

Dear Chris,
If you hadn't spoken to her she wouldn't have known you exist. Have a great time.

Dear Pete,
I've just failed my exams. Probably because I went out too much with a super boy. Should I stop seeing him?

Angela Cox

Dear Angela,
You might have passed if you had worked harder. Why not ask him to help you work for the next exams?

II Verstehen und Reagieren

Zuordnen

Die Lernenden versuchen, Antwortschreiben von Pete den richtigen Absendern zuzuordnen. Folgende Texte erscheinen an der Tafel, auf dem Tageslichtprojektor oder auf einem Arbeitsblatt. Drei neue Briefe sind hinzugekommen, die Sie den Lernenden vorlesen.

1. You might have passed if you had worked harder.

2. If you had written your name on them nobody would have stolen them.

3. You wouldn't have this problem if you hadn't stayed out late.

4. If you had gone away together you might both have been unhappy.

5. It would have been worse if you hadn't told him.

6. If you hadn't spoken to her she wouldn't have known you exist.

7. She wouldn't be so annoyed if you had asked her first.

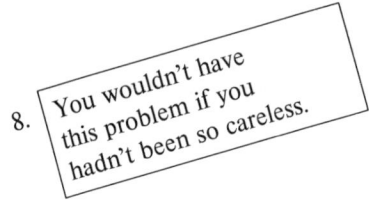

8. You wouldn't have this problem if you hadn't been so careless.

9. If you had left last year you might be very sorry now.

I stayed out late last night. Now my father won't let me go out for a week.
Dave Jones

My sister is annoyed because I wore her jeans last night without asking her. She won't speak to me.
Teresa Barnes

I've just told my boyfriend I don't want to see him any more. Now he's so unhappy. Was it right to tell him?
Carla Wright

L: Pete has so many letters to answer that he sometimes gets them mixed up. He's written all the answers and now he doesn't know which answer goes with which letter. Let's help him. What about number one: »You might have passed if you had worked harder.« Do we know who wrote that letter? Look, there are three more letters here – from Teresa Barnes, Carla Wright and Dave Jones. (Lesen Sie diese Briefe vor.) Which letter does answer number one go with?
S: Angela's.
L: And number two: »If you...«
    usw.

Lesen Sie nun alle Antwortschreiben der Reihe nach vor.
Lösungen:
1. Angela, 2. Sue, 3. Dave, 4. Jean, 5. Carla, 6. Chris, 7. Teresa, 8. Tony, 9. Don.

III Reproduzieren

Spekulieren
Die Schüler überlegen, wie sie in bestimmten Situationen gehandelt hätten. Schreiben Sie die vorgegebenen Situationen auf ein Arbeitsblatt bzw. an die Tafel oder auf den Tageslichtprojektor. Lesen Sie dann jeden Satz vor und sagen Sie, wie Sie gehandelt hätten, bevor Sie die Schüler um Stellungnahmen bitten.

Da *if*-Sätze dieser Art sehr lange geraten können, ist es ratsam, die Lernenden nur den Nebensatz mündlich reproduzieren zu lassen.

L: Sometimes a person does something and you think »If I had been him or her I wouldn't have done that« or »I would have done it differently«, don't you?

We're going to look at some situations like that now and think about what we would have done: whether we would have done the same as these people or whether we would have done something different.

Look at Jane, for example (lesen Sie den ersten Satz vor – s. unten): »Jane failed her exams, so she left school.«

I wouldn't have left school, would you? What about you, (S1)?

Als Hilfestellung können folgende Strukturen aufgeschrieben werden:

> I wouldn't have…, (either).
> I would/might have…, (too).

S1:   I wouldn't have left school, either.
L: And you, (S2)?
S2:   I would have left school, too.
S3:   I would have looked for a job.
      usw.

Ermuntern Sie die Lernenden dazu, nach unbekanntem Wortschatz zu fragen bzw. zu suchen. Die vorgeschlagenen Antworten in Klammern dienen nur Ihrer eigenen Orientierung.

1. Jane failed her exams, so she left school.
   (I would(n't) have left school/stayed at school; I would/might have looked for/ tried to find a job)
2. Liz lived in London. She was offered a good job in Scotland. But her boyfriend worked in London.
   (If I had been offered the job I would(n't) have taken it/would/might have look- ed for a job near London/asked my boyfriend to look for a job in Scotland);
   (If I had been the boyfriend I would(n't) have wanted Liz to take the job/would/ might have looked for a job in Scotland/a new girlfriend…)
3. Sue won £ 1000. She gave it to the church.
   (If I had won £ 1000 I would(n't)/might have given it to the church/to…/ bought…/spent it on…/gone on holiday…)
4. A homeless boy asked Pete for £ 2.
   (If he had asked me I would(n't)/might have given it to him/talked to him/asked him why he was homeless/tried to help him find somewhere to live…)
5. Alan's friend laughed at him in front of other people. Alan was very unhappy, but he didn't say anything.
   (If he had laughed at me I would have been unhappy, too/wouldn't have said anything either/would/might have talked to him later/asked him why he had

laughed at me/told him that he had hurt me/would/might never have talked to him again…)

6. Kevin took his small brother Tim shopping. Tim started to cry because Kevin wouldn't buy him any sweets. Everybody was looking.
(If he had been with me I wouldn't have bought him any sweets, either/would/ might have bought him the sweets/walked away/shouted at him/hit him/talked to him/bought him something else…)

7. Mike lent Ann a record, but she broke it.
(If I had lent it her/been Mike I wouldn't have said anything/would have asked her to buy a new one/would have been very angry…);
(If I had been Ann/broken it I would have bought a new one/would have given him the money for a new one/given him a present…)

8. Annette was invited to a party. When she arrived she saw that she was wearing the wrong sort of clothes.
(If I had done that/been Annette I would/might have gone home/wouldn't have stayed/would have borrowed some different clothes/sat in a corner all night/ laughed about it…)

IV Produzieren

Zuordnen

In Partner- oder Gruppenarbeit versuchen die Lernenden, die folgenden Satzpaare durch *if*-Sätze zu kombinieren, um ein Ereignis bzw. einen Zustand zu erklären. Es kann mündlich und/oder schriftlich gearbeitet werden.

L: Let's put these two lists together to explain what happened. Start with »if« and use the structures under the lists.

1. Sue did not write her name on her records	nobody would have stolen them
2. Jean and Sarah did not go on holiday together	they might have been unhappy
3. Chris looked at a pretty girl	he would not have walked into a wall
4. We did not bring a map	we would not have got lost.
5. Jane did not work hard	she might have passed the exams
6. Tony asked Pete for £ 2	they would not be friends today
7. Ann broke Mike's record	they might still be friends
8. Joe got up early	he would have missed the train
9. Hassan stayed up late	he would not be tired now
10. Tina was not careful	she would not have had an accident
If… had (written…) … had not (asked…)	

L: Let's do the first one together: If Sue had written her name on her records nobody would have stolen them.
Now go on.

Lösungen:
2. If Jean and Sarah had gone on holiday together they might have been unhappy.
3. If Chris had not looked at a pretty girl he would not have walked into a wall.
4. If we had brought a map we would not have got lost.
5. If Jane had worked harder she might have passed the exams.
6. If Tony had not asked Pete for £ 2 they would not be friends today.
7. If Ann had not broken Mike's record they might still be friends.
8. If Joe had not got up early he would have missed the train.
9. If Hassan had not stayed up so late he would not be so tired now.
10. If Tina had been (more) careful she would not have had an accident.

V Bewußtmachung

To speculate about things that <u>might have been different</u> under certain <u>conditions</u> we use

If + past perfect for the conditions +	**would/might have/would be**
If Jane **had worked** harder	she **might have passed** the exams.
If Hassan **had not stayed** up late	he **would not be** tired now.

Bemerkung:
<u>Would (have)</u> erscheint fast nie im <u>if</u>-Satz:
    If we **had brought** the map we would not have got lost.
    (Nicht: *If we **would have brought**...)
Wenn <u>would</u> nach <u>if</u> steht, drückt es meistens eine <u>Bereitschaft oder mangelnde Bereitschaft</u> aus:
    If everyone **would** give just a little money we could help the poor.
    The teacher said that **if** we **wouldn't do** our homework he would keep us in.

Indirect speech (1): reporting verb in past – back-shift

I Demonstration

Anhand eines Fragebogens zu Urlaubsplänen wird die indirekte Rede eingeführt.
Diese Lektion befaßt sich nur mit der Regel, daß *die Zeiten geändert werden, wenn
der Zeitbezug der direkten Rede vergangen ist und keine Auswirkung mehr auf die
Gegenwart hat.* Die Regel, daß die Zeiten erhalten bleiben, wenn der Zeitbezug der
direkten Rede noch zutrifft, wird in einer zweiten Lektion **Indirect speech** (2) behandelt.
Um die Lernenden nicht zu überfordern, wird nur kurz auf die Änderungen der
Personalpronomina eingegangen. Eine ausführlichere Behandlung erfolgt in **Indirect speech** (2).
Führen Sie den Fragebogen ein, indem Sie kurz über die Urlaubspläne der Lernenden sprechen.

L: Have you any plans for your next holiday? Are you going to go abroad or
   stay in your own country?
S1: I'm going to…
S2: . . .
   usw.
L: Do you want to learn the language of the country you'll visit or do you want
   to go somewhere where people understand your own language?
S: . . .
   usw.

Legen Sie den folgenden Fragebogen auf den Tageslichtprojektor, aber decken Sie
die Spalte **Yes total** zu.

Holidays – ten years ago			
Name: Kathleen Waters			
If the statement is true, say **yes**. If not, say **no**.	Yes	No	Yes total
1. I <u>am</u> going abroad for my next holiday.	☐	☒	25%
somewhere in my own country.	☒	☐	75%
to get a job in the holidays.	☐	☒	26%

2. I <u>want</u> to learn a foreign language for my holiday.	☐	☒	20%
go somewhere where people <u>understand</u> my own language.	☒	☐	60%
I only <u>want</u> to lie on a beach.	☒	☐	48%
3. I <u>have</u> been abroad.	☐	☒	34%
flown in a plane.	☐	☒	16%
travelled by boat.	☒	☐	40%
eaten foreign food.	☐	☒	35%
4. I <u>am</u> planning to visit different places.	☐	☒	32%
stay in one place.	☒	☐	68%
do a lot of sightseeing.	☐	☒	27%
read a lot of books.	☒	☐	83%

L: This is a questionnaire. It was given to people ten years ago to find out about their holiday plans. This questionnaire was filled in by someone called Kathleen Waters. Let's see what she said.

Verbalisieren Sie jede Antwort in der indirekten Rede. Schreiben Sie dabei die veränderten Verbformen und Personalpronomina an.

L: She said <u>she was</u> not going abroad for <u>her</u> next holiday.
She said she <u>was</u> going somewhere in her own country.
She said she <u>was</u> not going to get a job in the holidays.

She said she <u>did</u> not want to learn a foreign language for her holiday.
She said she <u>wanted</u> to go somewhere where people <u>understood</u> her own language.
She said she only <u>wanted</u> to lie on a beach.

She said she <u>had</u> not been abroad and she <u>had</u> not flown in a plane.
She said she <u>had</u> travelled by boat.
She also said she <u>had</u> not eaten foreign food.

She said she <u>was</u> not planning to visit different places, but that she <u>was</u> planning to stay in one place.
She said she <u>was</u> not planning to do a lot of sightseeing.
She also said she <u>was</u> planning to read a lot of books.

II Verstehen und Reagieren

Fragebogen auswerten
Decken Sie nun die Spalte **Yes total** auf.
   L: This questionnaire was given to a lot of people. Then they were collected to
       find out what most people said. So many people (deuten Sie auf die Prozent-
       sätze) answered each question with »yes«.
Fragen Sie in beliebiger Reihenfolge, wieviel Prozent der Befragten jede Aussage
bejaht haben.
   L: How many people said they had flown in a plane?
   S: Sixteen per cent.
   L: How many said they wanted to learn a foreign language for their holiday?
   S: Twenty per cent.
       usw.

III Reproduzieren

Fragebogen lesen
Teilen Sie jedem Schüler einen zweiten Fragebogen aus. In jeden Fragebogen ist
ein anderer Name eingetragen, und die Kästchen sind unterschiedlich angekreuzt.
Der folgende Fragebogen z.B. wurde von einem gewissen Steve Davies ausgefüllt.
Die Prozentzahlen sind überall gleich.

Holidays – two years ago			
Name: *Steve Davies*			
If the statement is true, say **yes**. If not, say **no**.	**Yes**	**No**	**Yes total**
1. I <u>am</u> going abroad for my next holiday.	☒	☐	60%
somewhere in my own country.	☐	☒	40%
to get a job in the holidays.	☐	☒	18%
2. I <u>want</u> to learn a foreign language for my holiday.	☒	☐	50%
go somewhere where people <u>understand</u> my own language.	☐	☒	46%
I only <u>want</u> to lie on a beach.	☐	☒	26%

3. I have been abroad.		☐	☒	65%
flown in a plane.		☒	☐	54%
travelled by boat.		☒	☐	28%
eaten foreign food.		☐	☒	46%
4. I am planning to visit different places.		☒	☐	57%
stay in one place.		☐	☒	33%
do a lot of sightseeing.		☒	☐	52%
read a lot of books.		☐	☒	43%

Geben Sie das Muster für jede Aussagegruppe vor, indem Sie die jeweilige Eintragung in Ihrem eigenen Fragebogen verbalisieren. Die Schüler lesen dann die entsprechenden Eintragungen in ihren Fragebögen vor. Als Hilfestellung können die folgenden Strukturen aufgeschrieben werden.

He She	said	he she	was (not) going (only) wanted to did not want to had (not) been abroad/flown… was (not) planning to	…

L: My questionnaire was filled in by (Sally Hardcastle). Who filled yours in, (S1)?
S1: (Steve Davies).
L: Sally said she was going abroad for her next holiday. What about Steve?
S1: He said he was going abroad, too.
L: And who filled yours in, (S2)?
S2: (Mike Johnstone).
L: What did he say?
S2: He said he was going somewhere in his own country.
usw.

Geben Sie den Schülern die Möglichkeit, ihre Eintragungen für die erste Aussagegruppe vorzulesen, bevor Sie das Muster für die zweite Aussagegruppe vorgeben.

L: Sally Hardcastle said she did not want to learn a foreign language for her holiday.
usw.

IV Produzieren

Fragebögen auswerten
Die Prozentsätze auf den zwei Jahre alten Fragebogen werden mit den zehn Jahre alten verglichen. Geben Sie für jede Aussagegruppe das Muster der ersten Aussage vor. Danach können die Lernenden alleine fortfahren.

L: This questionnaire was given to people two years ago and ten years ago. Let's see if there are any differences. Ten years ago twenty-five per cent said they were not going abroad for their next holiday. And two years ago?

S1: Sixty per cent said they were going abroad.
(Als Sprechimpuls deuten Sie auf die jeweiligen Zahlen.)

S2: Ten years ago seventy-five per cent said they were going somewhere in their own country.

S3: Two years ago forty per cent said they were not going ...
usw.

V Bewußtmachung

L: Look what Steve Davies said two years ago:
»I am going abroad for my next holiday.«
»I want to learn a foreign language for my holiday.«
»I haven't been abroad.«
»I am planning to visit different places.«
These are his exact words. We call this direct speech. When we tell someone else what Steve said we do not use his direct words. We report what he said indirectly. So we call this reported or indirect speech.
Now report Steve's direct words to me, but be careful of the tenses. You will have to change the words »I« and »my«, too. Steve said he...? (Deuten Sie auf die Muster, die Sie während der Phase III als Hilfestellung aufgeschrieben hatten.)

S: Was going abroad for his next holiday.

L: Yes, that's right. And he said he...?

S: Wanted to...
usw.

L: So when we report direct speech we have to change the pronouns, don't we? Can you give me some examples?
(Die Schüler führen Beispiele aus den zwei Fragebögen an: I – he/she, my – his/her.)
And we have to change the tenses. We change them like this.

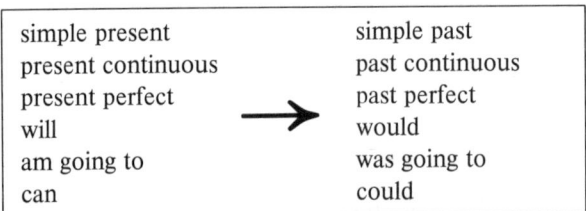

simple present	simple past
present continuous	past continuous
present perfect	past perfect
will	would
am going to	was going to
can	could

Für die direkte Rede im *simple past* und weitere Bemerkungen zur indirekten Wiedergabe vom *present perfect* s. **Indirect speech** (2), III Bemerkungen.

Indirect speech (2): reporting verb in past – back-shift or not?

Dieser Lektion sollte der erste Teil **Indirect speech** (1) vorausgegangen sein. In diesem zweiten Teil lernen die Schüler, daß bei der Wiedergabe von direkter Rede *die Zeiten nur dann geändert werden müssen, wenn der Zeitbezug der direkten Rede nicht mehr zutrifft. Ansonsten bleiben sie bestehen.* Da das Augenmerk nicht auf das Einschleifen einer neuen Struktur gerichtet ist, sondern auf die neue Anwendung einer bereits bekannten Struktur, findet die Bewußtmachung ausnahmsweise früher statt.

Um die Lernenden nicht zu überfordern, sollte auf Änderungen der Ortsangaben erst zu einem späteren Zeitpunkt eingegangen werden.

I Demonstration

Legen Sie folgende Folie auf den Tageslichtprojektor.

Past	← Direct speech →	Present or future
1. Mary said she couldn't do her homework. So Martin helped her.	Mary: »I can't do my homework.«	Mary said she can't do her homework. So I'm going to help her.
2. Gordon said he lived in Cardiff. But that was ten years ago. He might have moved.	Gordon: »I live in Cardiff.«	Gordon said he lives in Cardiff now.
3. When I saw Linda she told me she was starting a computer course the next day. But that was ages ago. She has probably finished it by now.	Linda: »I am starting a computer course tomorrow.«	Linda told me she is starting a computer course tomorrow. She is going to tell me about it tomorrow night.
4. Mrs Jones warned Tina that she would fail her exams the following summer if she didn't work harder. She was right. Tina failed.	Mrs Jones to Tina: »You'll fail your exams next summer if you don't work harder.«	Mrs Jones warned Tina that she will fail her exams next summer if she doesn't work harder. So Tina has decided to stay in and work every evening now.
5. Dave told me his bike had been stolen. He didn't know his brother had borrowed it.	Dave: »My bike's been stolen.«	Dave told me his bike has been stolen. He is going to tell the police.

Lassen Sie die Aussagen in der direkten Rede von Schülern vorlesen. Lesen Sie dann selbst die jeweils zwei verschiedenen Wiedergaben vor.

L: Can someone read the sentence in the middle, please? The one in direct speech.

S: »I can't do my homework.«

L: (Deuten Sie auf die jeweiligen Sätze.) Mary said she couldn't do her homework. So Martin helped her.
Mary said she can't do her homework. So I'm going to help her.
Can someone read the next sentence in direct speech, please?
usw.

II Verstehen und Reagieren

Hörverstehen: Zuordnen
Decken Sie die Spalten **Past** und **Present or future** zu, so daß nur die Überschriften sichtbar sind. Die Schüler ordnen die Wiedergaben in der indirekten Rede entweder der rechten oder der linken Spalte zu. Lesen Sie jeweils eine der beiden Wiedergaben der direkten Rede vor. Variieren Sie dabei die Reihenfolge der Wiedergaben mit geänderten und ungeänderten Zeiten.

Past	Direct speech	Present or future
zugedeckt	Mary: »I can't do my homework.«	zugedeckt

L: Now listen: »Mary said she can't do her homework. So I'm going to help her.« Now, when I report what Mary said, am I talking about Mary's past, present or future?

S: Her present.

L: That's right. It's *now* that she can't do her homework, isn't it?
(Decken Sie die zwei Wiedergaben der ersten Aussage in der direkten Rede auf und erklären Sie die zweite Wiedergabe):
»Mary said she couldn't do her homework. So Martin helped her.« When I say this I'm talking about Mary's past, aren't I?
(Lesen Sie nun eine der indirekten Wiedergaben der zweiten direkten Aussage vor, wobei Sie diese zwei Spalten zugedeckt lassen.)
»Gordon said he lived in Cardiff. But that was ten years ago. He might have moved.« Now, when I report this, am I talking about Gordon's past, present or future?
usw.
(Bei dem 5. Satz, rechte Spalte, erklären Sie, daß der Vorgang des Stehlens zwar in der Vergangenheit liegt, aber so nahe an die Gegenwart heranreicht,

daß er Auswirkungen auf die Gegenwart hat. Im Vergleich dazu liegt der Vorgang des Satzes in der linken Spalte so weit zurück, daß er in der Vergangenheit abgeschlossen ist und keine Auswirkungen mehr auf die Gegenwart hat.)

III Bewußtmachung

L: Compare these people's actual words (deuten Sie auf die mittlere Spalte) with the way the words are reported. Look what happens to the verbs. Let's find a rule to help us to report what other people say.

(Tafelanschrieb)
If the direct speech is about something which is in the **past** when we report it we ☐ change   the verbs.
☐ do not change
(Die Schüler schlagen vor, welches Kästchen anzukreuzen ist: *change.*)

Examples:
(Lassen Sie die Schüler selbst einige Beispiele aus der linken Spalte suchen.)
If the direct speech is about something which is still in the **present or future** when we report it we ☐ change   the verbs.
☐ do not change
(*do not change* wird angekreuzt.)
Examples:
(Rechte Spalte)

L: If we have to change the verbs we change them like this:

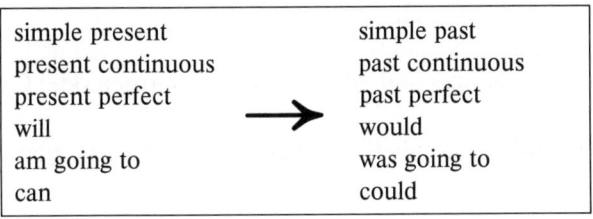

simple present	simple past
present continuous	past continuous
present perfect	past perfect
will	would
am going to	was going to
can	could

Die Schüler können einige Beispiele aus der Demonstrationsphase anführen, z.B.

can → could: Mary: »I <u>can't</u> do my homework.«
        Mary said she <u>couldn't</u> do her homework. So Martin helped her.
usw.

Bemerkungen:

1. Wörtliche Rede im *simple past*

Weisen Sie die Schüler auf folgenden Sonderfall hin: Wenn die wörtliche Rede im *simple past* steht, kann das *simple past* bei der Wiedergabe in der indirekten Rede zu *past perfect* geändert werden. Es *unterbleibt aber immer häufiger,* besonders dann, wenn der in der wörtlichen Rede ausgedrückte Zustand oder Vorgang nicht so lange her ist:

Ken: »I *saw* Sue at a party.«

Ken told me he *saw/had seen* Sue at a party.

Mrs Thatcher's son: »I *was involved* in the deal... I *met* my mother...«

Mr Thatcher admitted (...) that he *was involved* in the 1981 deal and *met* his mother during her official visit to Oman (*Observer,* 15.2.84).

2. Wörtliche Rede im *present perfect*

Wenn der in der wörtlichen Rede ausgedrückte Zustand bzw. Vorgang nicht so lange her ist, bleibt das *present perfect* auch in der indirekten Wiedergabe bestehen:

Barry: »Jim *has* gone to live in France.«

Barry told me that Jim *has* gone to live in France (er ist erst vor kurzem weggezogen).

Barry told me that Jim *had* gone to live in France (er ist vor längerer Zeit weggezogen).

Wenn bei der indirekten Wiedergabe die Zeiten geändert werden, bedeutet es oft, daß der Berichtende an der Richtigkeit der Aussage zweifelt. Für nähere Ausführungen s. **Indirect speech** (3).

Veränderungen der Zeitangaben und der Personalpronomina

Nach der Behandlung der Zeiten lenken Sie die Aufmerksamkeit auf die Änderungen der Zeitangaben und der Personalpronomina.

    L: If we report what someone said we sometimes have to change the verbs. Look for some more changes and underline them (Partner- oder Gruppenarbeit).

Die Unterstreichungen werden anschließend auch auf der Folie vorgenommen.

Lösungen:

1. I – she, my – her, 2. I – he, 3. I – she, tomorrow – the next day, 4. you – she, your – her, next summer – the following summer, 5. my – his

Erklären Sie diese Änderungen und fügen Sie noch einige dazu:

    L: So if we report what someone said we often have to change the personal pronouns. Sometimes we have to change expressions of time, too. For example, instead of »tomorrow« we might have to say »the next day« or »the following day« or »last Monday«, if we know what day the person meant. Often we have to change the expressions of time like this:

now	– then, at that time
today	– that day, last Sunday, on May 2...
yesterday	– the day before, last Tuesday, on Friday...
tonight	– that night, last night, last Sunday, on...
this week	– that week
last month	– the month before, the previous month, last June, in August...
a few days ago	– a few days before, last Monday, on...
next year	– the next/following year, in 1989...

IV Reproduzieren

Berichten: Alternativfragen
Teilen Sie folgendes Arbeitsblatt aus.

Today is Friday, March 8

1. Christine, last Sunday: »I'm starting my driving lessons tomorrow.«
   Christine phoned me last Sunday.
   She told me she $\frac{\text{is} \ \square}{\text{was} \ \square}$ starting her driving lessons the next day.

2. Suzy, last Tuesday: »I'm starting my driving lessons next week.«
   Suzy phoned me last Tuesday.
   She said she $\frac{\text{is} \ \square}{\text{was} \ \square}$ starting her driving lessons next week.

3. Diane, last Friday: »I want to invite you to my party next month.«
   Diane phoned me last Friday.
   She said she $\frac{\text{wants} \ \square}{\text{wanted} \ \square}$ to invite me to her party next month.

4. John, last Friday: »I want to invite you to my party tonight.«
   John phoned me last Friday.
   He said he $\frac{\text{wants} \ \square}{\text{wanted} \ \square}$ to invite me to his party that night.

5. Dennis, three weeks ago: »I'll leave school if I fail the exams next week.«
   Dennis phoned me three weeks ago.
   He told me that he $\frac{\text{will} \ \square}{\text{would} \ \square}$ leave school if he $\frac{\text{fails} \ \square}{\text{failed} \ \square}$ the exams the following week.

---

6. Mario, last Sunday: »I'll leave school if I fail the exams next summer.«
   Mario phoned me last Sunday.

   He told me that he $\frac{\text{will} \ \square}{\text{would} \ \square}$ leave school if he $\frac{\text{fails} \ \square}{\text{failed} \ \square}$ the exams next summer.

7. Tony, about two years ago: »I've left school. I've got married.«
   Tony phoned me about two years ago.

   He told me that he $\frac{\text{has} \ \square}{\text{had} \ \square}$ left school and that he $\frac{\text{has} \ \square}{\text{had} \ \square}$ got married.

8. Tim, last Sunday: »I've got married.«
   Tim phoned me last Sunday.

   He told me he $\frac{\text{has} \ \square}{\text{had} \ \square}$ got married.

9. Barbara, last Wednesday: »I can't come to the concert next Saturday.«
   Barbara phoned me last Wednesday.

   She said she $\frac{\text{can't} \ \square}{\text{couldn't} \ \square}$ come to the concert tomorrow.

10. Jeff, last Friday: »I can't come with you tomorrow night.«
    Jeff phoned me last Friday.

    He said he $\frac{\text{can't} \ \square}{\text{couldn't} \ \square}$ come with us the following night.

11. Lynne, a few weeks ago: »I started work two months ago.«
    Lynne phoned me a few weeks ago.

    She told me she $\frac{\text{started} \ \square}{\text{had started} \ \square}$ work two months before.

12. Katie, last Monday: »You left your purse here last night.«
    Katie phoned me last Monday.

    She told me I $\frac{\text{left} \ \square}{\text{had left} \ \square}$ my purse at her house the night before.

Lesen Sie immer beide indirekten Wiedergaben vor. Die Lernenden versuchen, die richtige Wiedergabe zu erkennen.

L: Look at what Christine said last Sunday. Listen – which is correct? (Lesen Sie beide indirekten Wiedergaben vor.)

S: Christine said she was starting her driving lessons the next day.

L: That's right. She's not starting tomorrow, on Saturday, is she? You could also say, »She said she was starting her driving lessons last Monday.« Let's put a cross in the box next to was.
    usw.

Lösungen:

1. was, 2. is, 3. wants, 4. wanted, 5. would... failed, 6. will... fails, 7. had... had, 8. has (*had* wäre nicht falsch, aber unnatürlich, vgl. III Bemerkungen), 9. can't,

10. couldn't, 11. started/had started (vgl. III Bemerkungen), 12. left/had left (vgl. III Bemerkungen. Hier bietet sich auch die Gelegenheit an, kurz auf die Änderung der Ortsangaben einzugehen.)

V Produzieren

Interview als Bericht abfassen
Ein Interview in direkter Rede wird in einen Bericht umgeschrieben. Dabei müssen sich die Lernenden entscheiden, in welchen Fällen ein geänderter Zeitbezug Änderungen der direkten Rede erforderlich macht. Das folgende Arbeitsblatt ist für Gruppen- oder Partnerarbeit gedacht.

Rich old Mr Moneybags was murdered sometime during the evening of Friday, March 18. The police do not yet know the exact time. The following day Inspector Braine is interviewing everyone in the house.

Inspector: Where <u>were</u> you yesterday evening, Mrs Moneybags?

Mrs M: I <u>was</u> out. After tea I <u>rang</u> a friend. I <u>can</u> tell you exactly what we <u>said</u>. I said, »<u>It's</u> a nice evening, Juliette dear. <u>I'd</u> like to go for a walk. What about you?«
Juliette answered, »I <u>can't</u> I'm afraid. <u>I'm</u> baby-sitting for my sister. She <u>goes</u> to night school on Fridays now.« So I <u>went</u> for a walk by myself. You see, Inspector, I remember our exact words.

Inspector: Thank you very much, Mrs Moneybags. Now, Mrs Kleenit you came here to clean yesterday, didn't you? Do you remember what time you <u>arrived</u>?

Mrs K: I <u>don't</u> know. Colin <u>will know</u>. <u>He's</u> always here when I <u>arrive</u>.

Colin: I <u>think</u> she <u>arrived</u> just before five. She <u>has</u> been coming later <u>this week</u>.

Inspector: And you, sir? Where <u>were</u> you <u>last night</u>?

Colin: Me? Well, <u>I've</u> had a lot of work to do <u>this week</u>. So <u>yesterday evening</u> I <u>decided</u> to relax. I <u>went</u> for a bike ride. That was from seven to a quarter to eight. So, you see, I <u>can't</u> have killed my uncle, can I? I <u>was</u> out.

Inspector: I see. Well, Colin, that was extremely helpful. I'm arresting you for the murder of your uncle, Mr Julian Moneybags.

Colin: <u>What! But how did you know? I mean… I didn't…!</u>

When the Inspector got back to his office he wrote his report. Help him to complete it. Be careful how you report the underlined words. You will need these words, too: was surprised, Mr Moneybags' nephew. Can you finish the last sentence to explain how the Inspector knew who the murderer was?

Report on the murder of Mr J. Moneybags   19.3.90

Mr J. Moneybags was murdered sometime during the evening of March 18. This morning I interviewed everyone in the house.
First I asked Mrs Moneybags where she......... yesterday evening. She told me she......... out. She said that after tea she......... a friend. She said she......... tell me exactly what they......... She suggested that since it......... a nice evening she......... like to go for a walk.
Her friend said she......... because she......... baby-sitting for her sister. She said her sister......... to night school on Fridays. Mrs Moneybags told me that she......... for a walk by herself.
Then I questioned the cleaner, Mrs Brenda Kleenit. When I asked her what time she......... yesterday she said she......... know. She told me that Colin, ..., ... know. She said he......... always at home when she......... Colin......... she......... just before five. He added that she......... been coming later.........
When I asked Colin where he......... last night he explained that he......... had a lot of work to do......... So................... he......... to relax and......... for a bike ride. He explained that he......... have killed his uncle because he......... out at the time of the murder. I arrested Colin. He.................. that I knew it was him.
I simply asked him how he knew ....

Lösungen:
was – was – rang (had rung) – could – said – was – would;
couldn't – was – goes – went;
arrived – didn't – Mr Moneybags' nephew – would – is – arrives;
thought – arrived – has – this week;
was – has – this week – yesterday evening – decided – went/go – could not – was;
was surprised;
what time his uncle was killed.

Indirect speech (3): reporting verb in past – back-shift expresses disbelief

Dieser Lektion sollten **Indirect speech** (1) und (2) vorausgegangen sein. In diesem dritten Teil gewinnen die Schüler die Einsicht, daß *geänderte Zeiten* bei der Wiedergabe von direkter Rede *darauf hinweisen können, daß der Berichtende an der Richtigkeit der Aussage zweifelt*. Da es hier nur um eine neue Anwendung bereits bekannter Strukturen geht, findet die Bewußtmachung ausnahmsweise früher statt.

I Demonstration

Der folgende Brief einer Jugendgruppe bezieht sich auf Wahläußerungen eines Abgeordneten in indirekter Rede. Erläutern Sie kurz den Hintergrund des Briefes.

L: In an English town, before the elections, the politicians made a lot of promises to the young people. After the elections the young people waited to see what would happen. They waited for a few weeks, but nothing happened. So they waited a bit longer. Still nothing changed. After one year they decided to write to their Member of Parliament and ask him about the promises he had made before the election. This is what they wrote.

Lesen Sie den Brief, der auf die rechte Hälfte einer Folie oder eines Arbeitsblattes geschrieben ist, vor.

Dear sir,

It is now a year since you won the election. What about all those promises you made to the young people here?

1. You told us we could have a room for a youth club. You said the town did not need the old factory and that we could have it. Did you mean it?

2. You said the government had promised the town money for youth projects. Is that true?

3. You told us you were planning a sports centre and that you had already talked to the government about it. Is that right?

4. You said you were going to build a swimming pool and that you wanted to start a football club. Can we still believe you?

5. You said, too, that the cinemas were going to show more films for young people.

6. You promised that we would have more teachers and that there would be more jobs for young people. You were thinking about an exchange programme with different countries, too.

7. Finally, you told us that you understood the problems of black kids here. But we are not really sure if you do.

When are you going to start keeping all these promises?

Yours faithfully,

Jane Greyson, Mike Taylor
(Youth Committee)

II Verstehen und Reagieren

Sprachäußerungen vergleichen

Die Schüler versuchen nun, aus diesem Brief die in der direkten Rede gemachten Versprechungen des Abgeordneten herauszufinden.

Lesen Sie den Brief noch einmal vor und tragen Sie die Versprechungen in der direkten Rede gegenüber den jeweiligen indirekten Äußerungen ein.

L: Now listen to the letter again. This time think of what the MP actually said when he made those promises. Look at the first promise:
»You told us we could have a room for a youth club.«
What did the MP probably say?

S: »You can have a room for a youth club.«

L: Yes. Let's write that down.
usw.

1. »You <u>can</u> have a room for a youth club.« »The town <u>doesn't</u> need the old factory. You <u>can</u> have it.« usw.

1. You told us we <u>could</u> have a room for a youth club. You said the town <u>did not</u> need the old factory and that we <u>could</u> have it. Did you mean it? 2. You said…

Lösungen

2. »The government <u>has</u> promised the town money for youth projects.«
3. »We <u>are</u>/I <u>am</u> planning a sports centre. We/I <u>have</u> already talked to the government about it.«
4. »We <u>are</u> going to build a swimming pool and we <u>want</u> to start a football club.«
5. »The cinemas <u>are</u> going to show more films for young people.«
6. »You <u>will</u> have more teachers and there <u>will</u> be more jobs for young people. We <u>are</u> thinking about an exchange programme with different countries.«
7. »We <u>understand</u> the problems of black kids here.«

Machen Sie nun auf die veränderte Zeitenfolge in der indirekten Rede aufmerksam:

L: These sentences (deuten Sie auf die linke Spalte) are the MP's exact words. We call this <u>direct speech</u>.
These sentences (deuten Sie auf die rechte Spalte) also tell us what the MP said, but they tell us indirectly. They are not his exact words. They are reported by someone else. So this is called <u>indirect</u> or <u>reported</u> speech.
Look at the tenses in the direct speech and in the indirect speech. Let's underline them.

Deuten Sie nun auf die veränderten Personalpronomina hin:

L: What other changes do you have to make when you report what someone else said?

S: »You« becomes »we«.

usw.

Die veränderten Personalpronomina werden ebenfalls unterstrichen.

III Reproduzieren

Sprachäußerungen vergleichen

Um die Funktion der indirekten Rede deutlich zu machen, werden jeweils zwei Sätze (Tafel, Tageslichtprojektor oder Arbeitsblatt) miteinander verglichen.

L: Look at these two sentences. Which one would make Ann happier?

(Lesen Sie beide Sätze vor):

1. Tony said Ann is very nice.

   Tony said Ann was very nice.

S: Tony said Ann is very nice.

Die Schüler können schon versuchen, die Unterschiede zwischen den jeweiligen Sätzen zu erklären.

Weitere Satzpaare:

2. Marion said she is moving to Sheffield.

   Marion said she was moving to Sheffield.

   Which sentence suggests she might not move?

3. Ken said he would lend you five pounds.

   Ken said he will lend you five pounds.

   Which sentence suggests you might not get the money?

4. Sue told me she wants to learn to drive.

   Sue told me she wanted to learn to drive.

   Which sentence suggests she still wants to learn/has not changed her mind?

5. Jean told me her boyfriend was working in Manchester.

   Jean told me her boyfriend is working in Manchester.

   Which sentence makes you ask if he is still working there?

6. Eric told me that Maria had bought a motor bike.

   Eric told me that Maria has bought a motor bike.

   Which sentence makes you ask if it is really true?

7. Ann said that Jeff is having a party on Saturday.

   Ann said that Jeff was having a party on Saturday.

   Which statement do you believe more?

Lösungen:

2. ... was moving, 3. ... would lend, 4. ... wants, 5. ... was working, 6. ... had bought, 7. ... is having.

IV Bewußtmachung

Erklären Sie die Regel.

L: When people report what someone said they sometimes want to show that they don't quite believe it.

To show this they $\begin{array}{l}\square \text{ change} \\ \square \text{ do not change}\end{array}$ the tenses of the direct speech.

(*change* wird angekreuzt).

Weisen Sie darauf hin, daß im Deutschen solche Zweifel oft durch »würde« ausgedrückt werden, und warnen Sie die Lernenden davor, im Englischen das naheliegende *would* zu benutzen,

z.B.

John sagte, er *arbeitet* beim Zirkus.
John said he *works* at the circus.

John sagte, er *würde* beim Zirkus arbeiten.
John said he *worked* at the circus. (Nicht *would work,* eine Struktur, die es im Englischen zwar gibt, die aber eine andere Bedeutung hat, nämlich: »John sagte, er *wäre bereit,* beim Zirkus zu arbeiten.«)

Machen Sie auch darauf aufmerksam, daß im Englischen kein Komma vor dem Nebensatz steht.

Die Schüler können entweder Beispiele aus Phasen II und III zitieren oder versuchen, in Partner- oder Gruppenarbeit eigene Beispiele zu finden.

V Produzieren

Sprachäußerungen vergleichen

Paarweise üben die Schüler Minidialoge, bei denen sie entscheiden müssen, ob die Anfangsaussage ernst zu nehmen ist oder nicht. Ein Dialogmuster hilft ihnen bei der Auswahl der richtigen sprachlichen Reaktionen. Ermutigen Sie die Lernenden dazu, die Dialoge zu erweitern, z.B. durch weitere Kommentare, Begründungen usw.

Jedes Paar bekommt Arbeitsblatt A für den einen und B für den anderen Partner. Abwechselnd fängt jeder Partner einen Minidialog an:

Partner A	Partner B
Find a partner. Start a conversation by saying the following sentence to your partner: 1. Sue told me she <u>is</u> leaving school.	This will help you to answer: I see. That's interesting. (When/Why?…) Great. But you don't | believe her/him? | think she/he will? 1. That's interesting. When?
(Think of an answer.)	Now YOU start the next conversation: 2. Anna said she <u>can</u> get me a job.
2. This will help you to answer: I see. That's interesting. (When/Why?…) Great. But you don't | believe her/him? | think she/he will? Now YOU start the next conversation: 3. Dave told me he <u>was</u> learning French at night school. …	3. But…? 4. Kevin said he <u>has</u> to stay in tonight.
4. … 5. Derek said he <u>would</u> come to our party.	5. … 6. Phil told me he <u>wanted</u> to buy a motor bike.
6. … 7. Maria told me she <u>is</u> taking a computer course.	

8. ...
9. Hassan told me he <u>was</u> leaving school.

10. ..
11. Eva told me she <u>is</u> learning Italian at night school.

12. ...
13. Martin said he <u>will</u> come to our party.

14. ...
15. Chris told me he <u>was</u> taking driving lessons.

16. ...

If you want more practice exchange sheets with your partner and start again.

7. ...
8. Lynne told me she <u>had</u> stopped smoking.

9. ...
10. Diane said she <u>could</u> get me a job.

11. ...
12. Annette said she <u>had</u> to stay in tonight.

13. ..
14. Helen told me she <u>wants</u> to buy a computer.

15. ...
16. Barry told me he <u>has</u> stopped smoking.

If you want more practice exchange sheets with your partner and start again.

Einige Paare können nun ausgewählte Minidialoge der Klasse vorführen.

-Ing form as object (gerund)

 Name: _Malcolm Jones_

I like reading and playing football. I enjoy dancing, too. I have just started learning judo.

 Name: _Dennis Thomson_

I like playing football and I enjoy reading. I'm good at running. I have just started learning judo. I hate helping my mother at home.

 Name: _Mike Branston_

I like swimming. I'm good at running, but not very good at jumping. I like dancing.

 Name: _Roger Curtis_

I like swimming and I enjoy playing football. I have just started learning judo. I hate doing homework.

 Name: _Andy Jennings_

I enjoy playing football and reading. I love listening to pop music. But I don't like doing homework and I hate helping my mother at home.

 Name: _Keith Hartnell_

I like swimming and dancing and I love listening to pop music. I'm good at running, but not so good at jumping.

I Demonstration

Führen Sie die Folie ein, indem Sie kurz über *penfriends* oder *hobbies* sprechen. Besprechen Sie dann die Folie.

L: Look, these boys all go to a British school. They're learning German and they're looking for German penfriends. They've written a few sentences about themselves. Their teacher will give this information to some German pupils. Then the Germans can choose someone with the same interests for a penfriend.

Look at Malcolm Jones, for instance. He tells us, »I like reading and…«
usw.
Lesen Sie alle »Steckbriefe« vor.

II Verstehen und Reagieren

Geheime Auswahl
Suchen Sie einen der Jungen als »Ihren Brieffreund« aus und beschreiben Sie zwei
seiner Interessen, ohne aber seinen Namen preiszugeben. Die Lernenden versuchen, seinen Namen herauszufinden, wobei die Zahl ihrer Versuche auf drei beschränkt wird. Diese Aktivität kann auch als Mannschaftswettbewerb organisiert
werden.

L: One of these boys is my English penfriend. Can you guess who? Listen, I'll
help you: He likes swimming and he's good at running. You can ask me
three questions. Ask questions like, »Is it Andy?« – »Is it Roger?« and so on.

S1: Is it Mike?

L: No, try again.

S2: Is it Keith?

L: Yes, that's right. (One point for your team.)
Now I have a different penfriend. Listen again: He…
usw.

III Reproduzieren

Geheime Auswahl
Das Sprachmuster wird nicht verbal, sondern schriftlich vorgegeben, indem die
Lernenden die Beschreibungen auf der Folie vorlesen dürfen. Das Ratespiel wird
fortgesetzt, allerdings suchen sich diesmal die Schüler und nicht die Lehrkraft einen »Brieffreund« aus.

L: Now I want one of you to choose a penfriend.
(S1), tell us two things about your »penfriend«.

S1: He enjoys playing football. He hates helping his mother at home.
usw.

IV Produzieren

Information erfragen und erteilen
Die Schüler geben Auskunft über sich selbst.

L: Now we know something about all these boys. But what about you people here? Tell me something about yourselves.

Schreiben Sie als Hilfestellung folgende Strukturen an. Ermuntern Sie die Lernenden, möglichst viele Verben zu verwenden. Es kann auch hilfreich sein, weiteren Wortschatz vorzuschlagen.

> I like/enjoy/love/hate …ing.
> I'm good at/not very good at …ing.
> I've just started …ing (…).

Je nach Leistungsstand können die Lernenden sich gegenseitig Fragen stellen. Vermeiden Sie aber die Frage *What do you like doing?,* da sie zu diesem frühen Zeitpunkt zu Falschaussagen wie **I like doing swimming* führen kann.

S1: (S2), do you like listening to records?
S2: Yes, (but only pop music). (S3), are you good at swimming?
S3: No, (but I'm good at running). (S4), …?
    usw.

V Bewußtmachung

After these verbs we use the -ing form:

> like/enjoy/love/hate/start + -ing

Also

> good at + -ing

Lassen Sie einige Beispiele aus der vorausgegangenen Lektion aufschreiben.

Modal: can (permission): you can/can't

Legen Sie folgende Folie auf den Tageslichtprojektor.

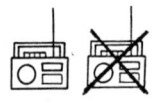 can / can't listen to your radio

 can / can't play records

 can / can't play football

 can / can't ride a bike

 can / can't make a fire

 can / can't take your dog with you

 can use the kitchen

 can use the washing machines

 can't smoke

I Demonstration

Die Symbole unterhalb der Diagramme stellen Ge- und Verbote in sechs verschiedenen Jugendherbergen dar. Erklären Sie die Symbole wie folgt:

L: When some young people go on holiday they stay at youth hostels. Look, here are six youth hostels: Riverside, Norton, Green Fields, Sunnylands, Hill House and Golden Sands.
Look at Riverside. These pictures tell you what you can do and what you can't do: You can listen to your radio, you can play records, you can play football. But you can't ride a bike. You can use the kitchen...
usw.

II Verstehen und Reagieren

Auskunft erteilen

L: You can take your dog to some hostels. You can take it to...?
S1: Norton.
S2: And Green Fields.
S3: And Sunnylands.
L: That's right. In some hostels you can't ride a bike.
S4: Riverside.
   usw.

Vermeiden Sie die Frageform *Where can you (play football...)?*, da sie zu diesem frühen Zeitpunkt Verwirrung stiftet. Anstatt dessen benutzen Sie die Formulierung, *In some hostels you can/can't...*

III Reproduzieren

Auskunft erteilen
Die Vorschriften der einzelnen Jugendherbergen für den jeweils selben Bereich werden miteinander verglichen.

L: You can listen to your radio at Riverside. But you can't listen to it at Green Fields. And the other hostels?
S1: You can listen to it at Norton.
S2: You can't listen to it at Sunnylands.
   usw.
L: You can play records at Riverside. But you can't play them at Sunnylands. And the other hostels?
S3: You can't play records/them at Hill House.
   usw.

IV Produzieren

Auskunft erteilen

L: Now I want two people to come out here. You (S1) work at an information office. You (S2) want some information about youth hostels. Say, »Tell me about the youth hostels, please.«

S2: Tell me about the youth hostels, please.

L: (Deutet auf die verschiedenen Jugendherbergen samt ihren Vorschriften): There's Riverside. You can listen to your radio there. You can play records. Now you (S1) give him/her this information. Start again: There's Riverside...

S1: There's Riverside. You can listen to your radio. You can...

In Partnerarbeit üben die Lernenden solche Dialoge. Nach der Informationsvermittlung über eine bestimmte Jugendherberge werden die Rollen zwischen Fragendem und Auskunftgebendem vertauscht.

Als weitere Übung können die Schüler in Partner- oder Gruppenarbeit eigene Symbole erfinden, z.B. für die Hausordnung in der Schule. Sie können auch lustige, ungewöhnliche Vorschläge machen.

V Bewußtmachung

To say that it is or is not possible to do something we use

can (not)	+ infinitive
You **can**	**play** football.
You **cannot/can't**	**smoke.**

Modal: have to: affirmative

Legen Sie folgende Folie auf den Tageslichtprojektor.

A. She/he has to...

I Demonstration

L: Mr and Mrs Collins have three children, Roger, Sandra and Paul. This weekend the parents are going away. Before they go they give the children a list of jobs. Let's see what these jobs are. (Zeigt auf die Pflichten für Samstag bzw. Sonntag): These are the jobs for Saturday and these are the jobs for Sunday.

(Um die Schwierigkeiten zu isolieren, sollte der Fragetyp *What does Roger have to do?* zu diesem Zeitpunkt noch vermieden werden. Ebenso sollte die Formulierung *Let's see what Roger has to do* noch nicht verwendet werden, da sie zu der Falschaussage* »He has to do clean up...« führen kann.)
Let's see what Roger's jobs are on Saturday. He has to clean up the living room. He has to...
usw.
Now let's see what Sandra's jobs are on Saturday.
She has to make the beds.
She has to...
usw.
(Die Pflichten von Sandra und Paul werden besprochen.)

II Verstehen und Reagieren

Auskunft erteilen

L: There are a lot of jobs for the children to do this weekend, aren't there? Let's see (deutet auf die linke Reihe von Symbolen unterhalb der Tabelle): Somebody has to clean up the living room. Who's that?

S1: Roger.

L: Who has to post the letters?

S2: Sandra.

usw.

Fragen Sie nach den weiteren Aufgaben, die nur einmal und von nur einer Person an diesem Wochenende gemacht werden sollten: *fetch the paper, clean the bird cage, water the plants.*

III Reproduzieren

Auskunft erteilen

L: Let's look at Roger's jobs. (Deutet auf die Pflichten Rogers für Samstag): On Saturday he has to clean up the living room. He has to feed the cat, too. He has to get a meal ready. Then he has to set the table. And after that he has to do the washing up.
What about Sunday? On Sunday...? (Schreiben Sie *He has to...* als Hilfestellung auf.)

S1: He has to make the beds.

S2: He has to...

usw.

In ähnlicher Weise werden Sandras Pflichten für das ganze Wochenende verbalisiert.

IV Produzieren

Auskunft erteilen
- L: Now tell me about Paul's jobs for the weekend.
- S1: He has to fetch the paper.
- S2: He has to get a meal ready.
  usw.

B. They have to...

I Demonstration

Zunächst werden die Aufgaben, die am Samstag von mehr als einer Person zu verrichten sind, besprochen: *do the shopping, get a meal ready, set the table, do the washing up.* Dabei soll der Fragetyp *»Who has to...?«* vermieden werden. Es ist für die Schüler verwirrend, wenn eine Antwort mit *have to* gebildet werden soll.

- L: (Deutet auf die entsprechenden Symbole unterhalb der Tabelle): What about the weekend shopping? (Symbole: *do the shopping*, Samstag, Sandra, Paul): Oh yes, Sandra and Paul have to do the shopping.
  (Symbol: *get a meal ready* unterhalb der Tabelle): And what about meals? Oh, I see. They all have to get a meal ready. And what about setting the table? They all have to do that, too, don't they?
  And the washing up? Roger and Paul have to do that.

II Verstehen und Reagieren

Auskunft erteilen
Es werden nur die Aufgaben besprochen, die an beiden Tagen mehr als einmal zu verrichten sind: *feed the cat, make the beds, take the dog out, get a meal ready, set the table, do the washing up.*

- L: This weekend two people have to feed the cat.
- S1: Yes – Roger and Paul.
- L: And which people have to make the beds? (Nicht *Who has to...?*.)
- S2: Roger and Sandra.
- L: Which people have to... (take the dog out, get a meal ready, set the table, do the washing up)?
  usw.

III Reproduzieren

Falschaussagen

Machen Sie absichtlich falsche Aussagen über die Aufgaben, die am Samstag, am Sonntag oder an beiden Tagen zusammen von jeweils zwei oder drei Personen zu verrichten sind. Damit sich die Schülerantworten immer auf mehrere Personen beziehen *(They have to…),* suchen Sie Aufgaben heraus, die jeweils von mehr als einer Person gemacht werden müssen: *do the shopping, get a meal ready, set the table, do the washing up.* Machen Sie dann eine falsche Aussage über die Art der Aufgaben. Die Schüler korrigieren Sie, indem sie die Pflichten heraussuchen, die tatsächlich von den genannten Personen zu erfüllen sind. Dabei gibt es mehrere Möglichkeiten.

L: It's Saturday today. Sandra and Paul have to clean up the living room. Is that right?

S1: No. They have to (do the shopping/get a meal ready/set the table). (Schreiben Sie *They have to…* als Hilfestellung auf.)

L: Oh yes, that's right. What about Roger and Paul? They have to make the beds. Is that right?

S2: No. They have to (get a meal ready/set the table/do the washing up). usw.

Weitere mögliche »Falschaussagen«:

Saturday – Roger and Paul have to post the letters/take the dog out;
      Sandra and Paul have to feed the cat;
      Roger and Sandra have to fetch the paper/clean the bird cage;

Sunday   – Roger and Paul have to water the plants;
      Sandra and Paul have to make the beds/take the dog out;
      Roger and Sandra have to feed the cat;

This weekend – Sandra and Paul have to clean up the living room;
      Roger and Paul have to post the letters/water the plants;
      Roger and Sandra have to fetch the paper/clean the bird cage.

IV Produzieren

Gedächtnisspiel

L: Look at these pictures for a few minutes (deutet auf die Tabelle). Try to remember everyone's jobs. Don't write anything down. (Nach einigen Minuten wird die Klasse in zwei Gruppen geteilt und die Folie abgedeckt): Now we need two teams. Tell me about the children's jobs for the weekend. Start with one person, for example »Roger has to…« or »Paul has to…«. Or you can start with two people, for example »Roger and Sandra have to…«.

Or you can say, »They all have to…«. (Schreiben Sie diese drei Möglichkeiten als Hilfestellung auf.)
Let's start with team A.
(Abwechselnd versucht jede Mannschaft einen Satz zu bilden.)
Für richtige Antworten können Punkte vergeben werden.

V Bewußtmachung

To say that something is <u>necessary</u> we use

	have to + infinitive	
Sandra and Paul	**have to**	**do** the shopping.
Roger	**has to**	**take** the dog out.

Bemerkung:
Vorsicht bei der Übersetzung von »müssen« im Präsens! *Must* wird nur für sehr strikte Anweisungen und Verpflichtungen verwendet. *Have to* ist die gängigere Übersetzung. Deutsche neigen dazu, *must* allzu häufig zu gebrauchen, was aber für Briten sehr autoritär klingt.

Modal: must (logical consequence): must have passed/ be tired/be going out

	Why is John happy?		He must have passed his exam.
	Why is Linda tired?		She must have gone to bed late.
	Why is Kevin running?		He must have missed the bus.
	Why doesn't Jill answer the phone?		She must be asleep.
	Why is Colin so fat?		He must eat a lot of sweets.
	Why is it so noisy?		They must be having a party.
	Why is Sandra putting cases into her car?		She must be going on holiday.

I Demonstration

Führen Sie das Thema durch die Frage ein, weshalb die Schüler *happy, unhappy* oder *tired* aussehen.

    L: (S1), you look happy/unhappy today. You must have had a good/bad morning.

       (S2), you look tired. You must have gone to bed late.

       (Geben Sie den Schülern die Gelegenheit, kurz darauf einzugehen.)

Legen Sie die Folie auf den Tageslichtprojektor und lesen Sie die Sätze vor.

    L: Look at John. He's happy, isn't he? Why is he happy? – He must have passed his exam.

       And Linda? She looks tired, doesn't she? Why is she tired? – She must have…

       usw.

II Verstehen und Reagieren

Hörverstehen: Zuordnen
Legen Sie die folgende zweite Folie auf den Tageslichtprojektor. Die Schüler versuchen, Ihre Beschreibungen den Bildern zuzuordnen. Beschreiben Sie die Bilder jedoch nicht in der vorgegebenen Reihenfolge.

L: Listen. Let's see if you know which of these people I'm talking about. She has given up her job. She must have won a lot of money.
S1: Rose.
L: Yes, that's right. Try again.
He's taking his exams next week...
usw.

Bildbeschreibung:
Von oben nach unten und von links nach rechts
She has been travelling all day. She must be tired. (Mrs Lyons)
The phone is ringing. It must be...? (Simon)
She goes to work by bike now. She must have sold her car. (Helen)
There is a taxi in front of his house. He must be going away. (Mr Barker)
There is someone at the door. It must be...? (Brenda)
He does not live here any more. He must have moved. (Paul)
She knows a lot about films. She must go to the cinema a lot. (Penny)
He is taking his exams next week. He must be working very hard at the moment. (Ken)
She has given up her job. She must have won a lot of money. (Rose)
He has bought some French tapes. He must be learning French. (Barry)

III Reproduzieren

Hörverstehen: Zuordnen

Teilen Sie einen aus 34 Blatt bestehenden Pack Karten aus, auf denen folgende
Satzpaare stehen. Die Karten werden den Strukturen gemäß in Gruppen eingeteilt
und entsprechend numeriert:

Gruppe 1: *must have...*
Gruppe 2: *must be/eat/go/It must be ...*
Gruppe 3: *must be ...ing (present continuous)*
Gruppe 4: *must be ...ing (future)*
z.B.

| 1 Why is John happy? | | 1 He must have passed his exam. |

1 Why is Linda tired?   1 She must have gone to bed late.
1 Why is Kevin running?   1 He must have missed the bus.
1 Helen goes to work by bike now.   1 She must have sold her car.
1 Paul does not live here any more.   1 He must have moved.
1 Rose has given up her job.   1 She must have won a lot of money.

2 Why doesn't Jill answer the phone?   2 She must be asleep.
2 Mrs Lyons has been travelling   2 She must be tired.
   all day.
2 Why is Colin so fat?   2 He must eat a lot of sweets.
2 The phone is ringing.   2 It must be Simon.
2 There's someone at the door.   2 It must be the postman.
2 Penny knows a lot about films.   2 She must go to the cinema a lot.

3 Why is it so noisy?   3 Someone must be having a party.
3 Ken is taking his exams next week.   3 He must be working very hard.
3 Barry has bought some French tapes.   3 He must be learning French.

4 Why is Sandra putting cases   4 She must be going on holiday.
   into her car?
4 There's a taxi in front of   4 He must be going away.
   Mr Barker's house.

Behalten Sie aus jeder Gruppe ein passendes Satzpaar zurück. Geben Sie einem
Schüler (S1) die erste Karte dieses Satzpaares.

    L: (S1), read this out, please.
   S1:   Why is Kevin running?
    L: (Lesen Sie Ihren Satz vor.) He must have missed the bus.

Schüler, die glauben, einen Satzanfang der Gruppe 1 zu haben, lesen diesen jetzt vor.

L: Who has a sentence with number one on it?
     Which of you can start a conversation?

S2: Paul does not live here any more.

L: Who can say something about this?
     (Der Schüler mit der passenden Antwort liest sie vor.)

S3: He must have moved.

L: Who else has got a card with number one on it? Who can start the next conversation?

S4: Why is Linda tired?

S5: She must have gone to bed late.

Alle Schüler mit Karten der Gruppe 1 lesen ihre Sätze auf diese Weise vor.
Geben Sie dann das Muster für die Strukturen der Gruppen 2, 3 und 4 vor, bevor die Schüler versuchen, Satzpaare zu finden.

L: Who has a sentence with the number two on it? Who can begin a conversation?

usw.

Nach dem ersten Durchgang können die Karten neu verteilt werden, und das Frage-Antwort-Spiel kann wieder beginnen.

IV Produzieren

Hörverstehen: Zuordnen

Ganz ohne Hilfe der Lehrkraft versuchen die Schüler nun diese Minigespräche selbst durchzuführen.

L: That was very good. Now let's see if you can do it without my help. Who can start? Start with any number.

S1: Barry has bought some French tapes.

S2: He must be learning French.

S3: Why doesn't Jill answer the phone?

usw.

V Bewußtmachung

If it is **logical** that something
a) has happened
b) is happening or
c) is going to happen
we use

a)   **must have + past participle**

Why is John happy? He **must have**   **passed** his exam.

b)   **must + be**

Mrs Lyons has been travelling all day. She **must**   **be** tired.

or   **must be + ing**

Barry has bought some French tapes. He **must be** learning French.

c)   **must be + ing**

Why is Sandra putting cases into her car? She **must be** going on holiday.

In Partner- oder Gruppenarbeit suchen die Lernenden weitere Beispiele für jede Struktur.

Modals: must not/not have to

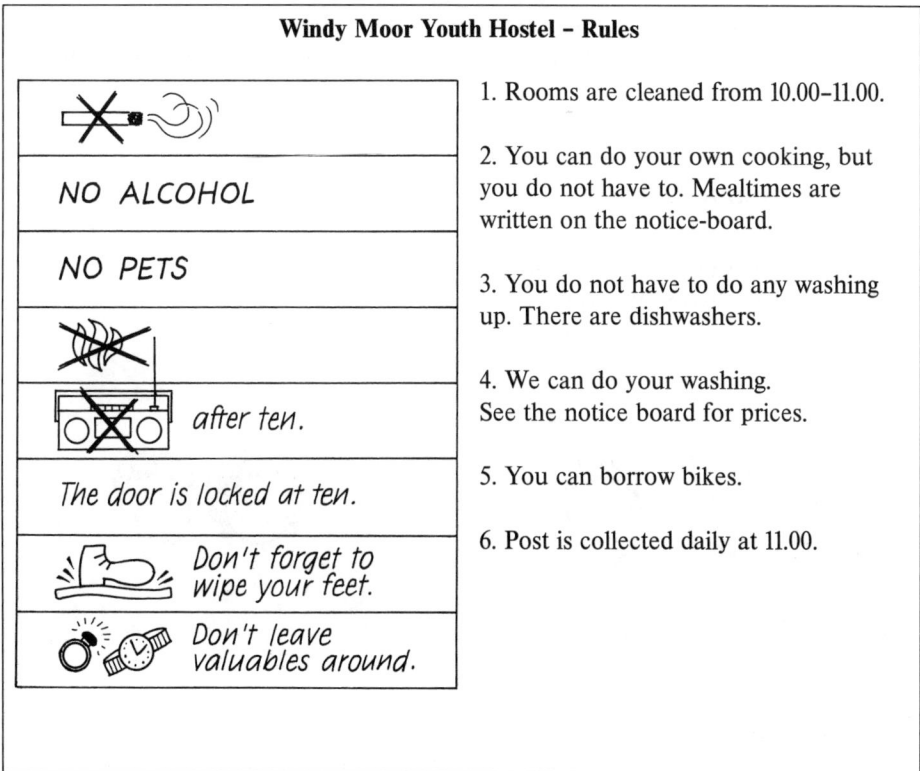

Windy Moor Youth Hostel – Rules

NO ALCOHOL	1. Rooms are cleaned from 10.00–11.00.
NO PETS	2. You can do your own cooking, but you do not have to. Mealtimes are written on the notice-board.
after ten.	3. You do not have to do any washing up. There are dishwashers.
The door is locked at ten.	4. We can do your washing. See the notice board for prices.
Don't forget to wipe your feet.	5. You can borrow bikes.
Don't leave valuables around.	6. Post is collected daily at 11.00.

I Demonstration

Führen Sie das Thema durch ein kurzes Gespräch über Jugendherbergen ein, z.B.

L: Has anyone ever stayed in a youth hostel? Where? Did you like it?
(Geben Sie den Schülern die Gelegenheit, kurz darauf zu antworten.)
Every youth hostel has a set of rules, doesn't it? They have to have rules if everyone is going to be happy.

Legen Sie die Folie auf den Tageslichtprojektor und erklären Sie die Hausregeln.

L: Look at the rules of this hostel.
You mustn't smoke. You mustn't drink alcohol. You mustn't bring pets. You mustn't make fires. You mustn't listen to your radio after ten o'clock. You mustn't forget to wipe your feet. You mustn't leave valuables around.
(Deuten Sie auf die Regeln in der rechten Spalte.)
But you don't have to clean your room.

And you don't have to do your own cooking.
You don't have to do any washing up.
You don't have to do your washing either, if you don't want to.
You don't have to bring your bike. You can borrow one.
And you don't have to take your letters to the post office. Someone will do it for you.

II Verstehen und Reagieren

Gedächtnisspiel: Information erfragen und erteilen
Teilen Sie folgendes Arbeitsblatt aus.

1. Can we smoke?	Val: Yes, you can.	☐
	Derek: No, you mustn't.	☐
2. Can we drink alcohol?	Val: No, you mustn't.	☐
	Derek: Yes, but you mustn't drink in your rooms.	☐
3. Can we take pets?	Val: No, you mustn't.	☐
	Derek: Yes, you don't have to ask.	☐
4. Can we make a fire?	Val: Yes, but it mustn't be near the hostel.	☐
	Derek: No, you mustn't.	☐
5. Can we take our radios?	Val: Yes, but you mustn't listen to them after ten o'clock.	☐
	Derek: Yes, but you mustn't listen to them in the evenings.	☐
6. What time do we have to be in at night?	Val: You mustn't stay out after ten.	☐
	Derek: You don't have to be in for a certain time.	☐

7. What about cleaning our rooms?	Val: You mustn't clean them before ten in the morning.	☐
	Derek: You don't have to clean them yourselves.	☐
8. Do we have to do our own cooking?	Val: You mustn't do any cooking.	☐
	Derek: You can if you want to, but you don't have to.	☐
9. What about the washing up?	Val: You don't have to do any washing up.	☐
	Derek: You have to do it yourselves.	☐
10. And our washing?	Val: You mustn't do any washing.	☐
	Derek: You don't have to do it yourselves if you don't want to.	☐
11. Is it a good place for bike rides?	Val: Super! And you don't have to take them with you. You can borrow them.	☐
	Derek: Marvellous! You mustn't forget to take them with you.	☐

L: Val and Derek have stayed at the Windy Moor youth hostel before. But these three people (links) haven't. So they're asking Val and Derek about the hostel. But it's a long time since Val and Derek were there and they can't remember it properly. Let's see if you can remember it better than they can. (Decken Sie die Folie zu.)
They ask, »Can we smoke?« Val tells them, »Yes, you can.« Derek says, »No, you mustn't.« Who's right?

S1: Derek.

L: Yes. So put a cross next to what Derek says.
Then they ask, »Can we drink alcohol?« Val says, »No, you mustn't.« Derek says, »Yes, but you mustn't drink in your rooms.« Who's right?

S2: Val.
usw.

Lösungen:
1. Derek, 2. Val, 3. Val, 4. Derek, 5. Val, 6. Val, 7. Derek, 8. Derek, 9. Val, 10. Derek, 11. Val.
Die Lösungen werden nun miteinander verglichen.

III Reproduzieren

Gedächtnisspiel: Information erfragen und erteilen
Bei abgedeckter Folie versuchen die Schüler, sich an die Hausregeln zu erinnern.
Geben Sie dabei das jeweilige Satzmuster vor.

    L: If someone asked you about the rules at Windy Moor youth hostel could
         you tell them? Is your memory better than Val's and Derek's? Let's see.
         What mustn't you do? You mustn't...?
    S1: Smoke.
    L: Yes, that's right. And...?
    S2: You mustn't make fires.
        usw.

Weitere Verbote in beliebiger Reihenfolge:
You must not drink alcohol/take pets/listen to the radio after ten/stay out after ten/
forget to wipe your feet/leave valuables around.

    L: And what don't you have to do at Windy Moor?
    S1: Clean your room.
    S2: You don't have to cook/do your own cooking.
        usw.

Weitere Antworten:
You do not have to do any washing up/do any, your own washing/take your bike/
go to, take your letters to the post office.

IV Produzieren

Information erfragen und erteilen
Zunächst werden in Gruppen- oder Partnerarbeit Verbote gesammelt, die für
Schule und Elternhaus gelten. Danach werden die Dinge zusammengestellt, die
man nicht zu machen braucht.

    L: Youth hostels have lists of things that you mustn't do. But there are things
         that you mustn't do at school and at home, too, aren't there? Write some of
         them down. (Ermutigen Sie die Schüler, nach unbekanntem Wortschatz zu
         fragen bzw. zu suchen.)

Diese Listen werden dann vorgelesen.

    S1: At school we mustn't be late.
    S2: We mustn't (forget our homework/talk/eat in class/fight in the play-
         ground/copy from our neighbours/leave our books at home/...).
    S3: At home I mustn't (get up late/watch too much TV/forget to clean my
         teeth, wash my hands before I eat/play loud music).
        usw.

L: And what about the things you <u>don't have to</u> do at school or at home? Make a list.

S1: At school we don't have to (wear uniform/go outside when it rains/…).

S2: At home I don't have to (help with the washing up/go shopping/make my bed/…).

V Bewußtmachung

Die Gefahr der deutschen Interferenz bei »must not« / »muß nicht« sollte herausgestellt werden.

Du <u>mußt/brauchst nicht</u> = You <u>don't have to</u>

Du darfst nicht = You mustn't

Die Schüler können folgende Beispiele übersetzen.

1. You mustn't come with me. (»Du darfst nicht…«)
   You don't have to come with me if you don't want to. (»Du mußt/brauchst nicht…«)
2. You mustn't go out today. You're ill. (»Du darfst nicht…«)
   You don't have to go out today. I'll post your letter for you. (»Du mußt/brauchst nicht…«)

Much, many, a lot of

Kevin	BE HEALTHIER	Philip

a lot of _____   *a lot of* _____

_____   _____

_____   _____

_____   _____

not many _____   *not many* _____

_____   _____

not much _____   *not much* _____

_____   _____

_____   _____

I Demonstration

Führen Sie das Thema Gesundheit ein, indem Sie kurz über gesunde Eß- und andere Lebensgewohnheiten sprechen. Dabei kann der Wortschatz (s. Lehrervortrag) eingeführt bzw. wiederholt werden.

L: How are you all this morning? Does anybody feel tired? – Why? Didn't you get much sleep last night? What time did you go to bed? (Geben Sie den Schülern die Gelegenheit, kurz darauf zu antworten.)
     If you want to be healthy it's important to get a lot of sleep, you know. What else do you have to do to be healthy?

S1: Eat fruit.

S2: Not eat sweets.
     usw.

Legen Sie die Folie auf den Tageslichtprojektor oder benutzen Sie die Tafel. Während Ihres Vortrags tragen Sie die unterstrichenen Wörter in die Tabelle für Kevin ein.

L: Look at these two men. Kevin doesn't look very healthy, does he? Philip looks a lot healthier. You see, Kevin eats a lot of sweets. (Tragen Sie *sweets* an der entsprechenden Stelle ein.) And he eats a lot of chocolate, too. He also has a lot of cake, a lot of chips, a lot of crisps and a lot of biscuits. He drinks a lot of beer, too and a lot of coke. He also has a lot of coffee.
He doesn't eat many apples, many oranges or many bananas. And he doesn't have many vegetables, either.
He doesn't eat much fruit at all. He doesn't drink much mineral water and he doesn't have much fruit juice, either. He doesn't get much exercise. And he always goes to bed very late, so he doesn't get much sleep.

II Verstehen und Reagieren

Tabelle ausfüllen
Teilen Sie ein Arbeitsblatt aus, auf dem die Tabelle für Kevin schon ausgefüllt ist (vgl. Folie), die für Philip aber noch nicht. Während Sie die zweite Tabelle auf der Folie ausfüllen, nehmen die Schüler die Einträge in ihren Arbeitsblättern vor.

L: So now we know why Kevin looks so unhealthy, don't we? But what about Philip? Why is he healthier than Kevin? Let's see: He eats a lot of fruit, especially oranges. He loves oranges. So let's write down »fruit« and »oranges« next to »a lot of«. He has a lot of vegetables, too. So let's write that down as well. He drinks a lot of mineral water and a lot of fruit juice. And, of course, he gets a lot of exercise and a lot of sleep.
He doesn't eat many sweets. So let's write »sweets« down next to »not many«. And he doesn't have many chips. He doesn't eat many crisps either. And he doesn't have many biscuits.
We can see why Philip is a lot healthier, can't we? What else?
He doesn't eat much chocolate. We'll write that down next to »not much«. He doesn't have much cake. He doesn't drink much beer or much coke. And he doesn't have much coffee, either.

III Reproduzieren

Tabellen vergleichen
Die zwei ausgefüllten Tabellen werden miteinander verglichen.

Kevin		Philip	
a lot of	sweets, chocolate, cake, chips, crisps, biscuits, beer, coke, coffee	a lot of	fruit, oranges, vegetables, mineral water, fruit juice, exercise, sleep
not many	apples, oranges, bananas, vegetables	not many	sweets, chips, crisps, biscuits
not much	fruit, mineral water, fruit juice, exercise, sleep	not much	chocolate, cake, beer, coke, coffee

Zuerst wird die Spalte *a lot of* bei Kevin besprochen.
L: So now we can see why Philip looks healthier than Kevin, can't we?
(Deuten Sie auf die Spalte *a lot of*): Kevin eats a lot of sweets and he...? (Als Sprechimpulse deuten Sie auf die jeweiligen Einträge.)
S1: Eats a lot of chocolate.
S2: He has a lot of...
usw.
L: And Philip? (Deuten Sie auf die Spalte *a lot of*.)
S1: He has a lot of fruit.
S2: He eats a lot of oranges.
usw.
In der gleichen Weise werden die weiteren Spalten besprochen. Geben Sie dabei die jeweilige Struktur vor:
L: (Spalte »not many« bei Kevin): Kevin doesn't eat many apples and he...?
S: He doesn't eat many...
usw.
(Deuten Sie auf die Spalte »not many« bei Philip.)
S: Philip doesn't eat many sweets.
usw.
L: Kevin doesn't eat much fruit. And?
S: He doesn't drink much mineral water.
S: Philip doesn't eat much...
usw.

IV Produzieren

Information erfragen und erteilen

Die Schüler geben Auskunft über ihre eigenen Lebensgewohnheiten. Dabei werden die neuen Strukturen gemischt. Ermutigen Sie die Schüler dazu, nach unbekanntem Wortschatz zu fragen bzw. zu suchen.

L: I don't eat many sweets, do you? What about you, (S1)? (Schreiben Sie als Hilfestellung folgende Strukturen an. Die zwei ausgefüllten Tabellen helfen bei der Zuordnung der Nomina zu *much* oder *many*.)

         I (eat/drink/have/get…) a lot of…

         I don't … much …

         I don't … many …

S1: I don't eat many sweets (either).

S2: I sometimes eat a lot of sweets.

     usw.

L: What about (exercise)?

S1: I get a lot of exercise.

     usw.

Da die Begriffe *a lot of, not many* und *not much* subjektiv sind, können die Schüler auch detaillierter nachfragen, z.B.

S: What is »not many sweets«? How many (packets) a day?/What do you mean by »…«? usw.

V Bewußtmachung

1. Not many – not much

Die Schüler versuchen herauszufinden, weshalb einige Nomina *many* zugeordnet werden, andere aber *much*. In Gruppen- oder Partnerarbeit versuchen sie, folgende Tabelle (auf dem Arbeitsblatt, vgl. II. Phase) auszufüllen.

not many	not much
apples, _____	fruit, _____
_____	_____
_____	_____

L: When we talked about Kevin and Philip we sometimes said »He doesn't eat much« of something and sometimes we said »He doesn't eat many«. For example, we said, »Kevin doesn't eat <u>many</u> apples«, then we said, »He doesn't eat <u>much</u> fruit«. Fill this table in and think about why we use <u>not many</u> with some words and <u>not much</u> with others. The tables we filled in before will help you.

not many	not much
apples, oranges, bananas, vegetables, sweets, chips, crisps, biscuits	fruit, mineral water, fruit juice, exercise, sleep, chocolate, cake, beer, coke, coffee

L: Look at the words under »not many«. They all have one letter that's the same.

S1: »s«

L: Yes. An »s« at the end of a word means that we can count the things: one apple, two apples etc.

For things we can **count** we use **not many**.

I don't eat **many** apples.

Look at the words »fruit« and »mineral water«. You can count apples, oranges and bananas, but you can't say »two fruits« or »three mineral waters«. You can only say »two tins of fruit« or »three bottles of mineral water«. For words like this we use **not much**.

For things we **can't count** we use **not much**.

I don't eat **much** fruit.

2. A lot of

L: We use »a lot of« for both countables and uncountables.

I eat <u>a lot of apples</u>.

I eat <u>a lot of fruit</u>.

Bemerkung:
In Großbritannien geht die Tendenz dahin, auch in Affirmativsätzen *a lot of* durch *much* bzw. *many* zu ersetzen.

122

Object + infinitive with »to« after certain verbs: she wants Bob to…

1
TELEGRAM
CAN BOB MEET ME AT STATION ?
Aunt Mary

2
Paul Go to cinema with me on Sat ?
Angela

3
ANN
Please ring me at 7.00
Mike

4
Sue
Concert starts at 7.30.
Don't be late.
Tony

5
NO SMOKING

6
DO NOT DRINK

7
NO SWIMMING NEAR ROCKS

8
CHILDREN CROSSING

9
NO DOGS IN THE PARK

10
NO PHOTOS

11
LIBRARY
QUIET PLEASE

12
SCHOOL NOTICE BOARD
Please remember :
School starts at 9.00, NOT 9.10.
Uniform is to be worn at all times.
Lock your bikes.

I Demonstration

Das Thema *notices and messages* kann eingeführt werden, indem Sie ein paar selbstgemachte Schilder und Notizzettel an die Tafel heften. Die Schilder sollen eher einen offiziellen Charakter haben, die Notizen einen privaten, z.B.

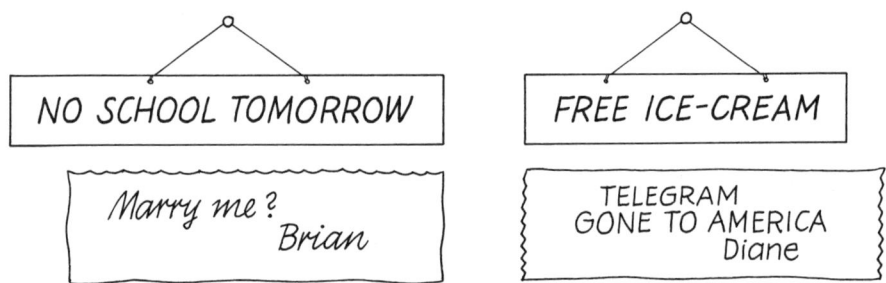

Heften Sie zunächst die offiziellen Schilder an die Tafel.

L: Look, I've brought some notices with me today. I'm afraid I have no ice-cream left, though and we'll have to ask the headmaster if the other notice is really true.

(Heften Sie nun die privaten Notizzettel an.) Now look at these messages or notes.

You can see how important it is to be able to understand notices and messages, can't you? And it's even more important when you're in a foreign country.

Legen Sie die Folie auf den Tageslichtprojektor oder benutzen Sie die Tafel.

L: Let's see if you can understand some notices and messages written in English.

Erklären Sie alle Schilder bzw. Notizen und schreiben Sie dabei die drei neuen Strukturen an (s. unten).

L: Look at this telegram (1). That's easy to understand, isn't it? Aunt Mary wants Bob to meet her at the station. (Schreiben Sie den Satz an.)
And this message? (2) Angela has invited Paul to go to the cinema with her on Saturday.
usw.

Weitere Erklärungen:

3. Mike asks Ann to ring him at seven.
4. Tony tells Sue not to be late. (Tafelanschrieb)
5. They tell you not to smoke. (Erklären Sie die »allgemeine« Bedeutung von *you.*)
They don't allow you to smoke. (TA)

124

6. They tell you not to drink this water.
   They warn you not to drink this water.
7. They warn you not to swim near the rocks.
8. They warn people to drive slowly.
   They warn people not to drive fast.
9. They don't allow people to take dogs into the park.
10. They don't want people to take photos.
11. They ask you to be quiet in the library.
    They don't want you to talk in there.
12. They don't expect you to be late.
    They expect you to wear uniform.
    They advise you to lock your bikes.

Während Ihres Vortrags entsteht folgendes Tafelbild:

A Aunt Mary | **wants** | Bob | **to** | meet her at the station.

(Lassen Sie Platz für 6 weitere Sätze)

B Tony | **tells** | Sue | **not to** | be late.

(Platz für 4 weitere Sätze)

C They | **do not allow** | you | **to** | smoke.

(Platz für 4 weitere Sätze)

II Verstehen und Reagieren

Sprachäußerungen Satzmustern zuordnen
Die Erklärungen, die Sie für die Schilder und Notizen gegeben haben (I »Weitere
Erklärungen«), werden den drei Sprachmustern zugeordnet.

   L: Look at the telegram again. Aunt Mary wants Bob to meet her at the station.
      I've called that »A«. Now look at Angela's note: Angela has invited Paul to
      go to the cinema with her. Do we put that under A, B or C?
   S: A.
   L: That's right. (Tragen Sie den Satz ein.) Now look at Mike's message: »Mike
      asks Ann to ring him at seven.« What sort of sentence is that: A, B or C?
      usw.

Auf diese Weise wird das Tafelbild wie folgt ergänzt:

A	Aunt Mary	**wants**	Bob	**to**	meet her at the station.
	Angela	**has invited**	Paul		go to the cinema.
	Mike	**asks**	Ann		ring him at seven.
	They	**warn**	people		drive slowly.
		ask	you		be quiet in the library.
		expect			wear uniform.
		advise			lock your bikes.

B	Tony	**tells**	Sue	**not to**	be late.
	They	**tell**	you		smoke.
					drink this water.
		warn	them		swim near the rocks.
					drive fast.

C	They	do not **allow**	you	**to**	smoke.
			people		take dogs into the park.
		want			take photos.
					talk.
		expect			be late.

III Reproduzieren

Schilder und Notizen lesen
Verwenden Sie das gleiche Sprachmuster, um einige der Schilder zu beschreiben.
Decken Sie die angeschriebenen Muster zu, damit die Lernenden sie nicht einfach
ablesen können. Geben Sie jeweils das Sprachmuster vor und schreiben Sie das
Verb an.

   L: Look at the telegram again: Aunt Mary wants Bob to meet her at the station.
       Now tell me about Angela's message.
       (Schreiben Sie das Verb *has invited* an.)
   S: Angela has invited Paul to go to the cinema with her.
   L: And this one? (3)
       usw.
       (Deuten Sie auf 3, 8, 11, 12 *uniform, bikes*.)
Weitere Schülerantworten:
   3. Mike asks Ann to ring him at seven.
   8. They warn people to drive slowly.

11. They ask you to be quiet in the library.
12. They expect you to wear uniform.
    They advise you to lock your bikes.

    L: (Deuten Sie auf 4) Look at Tony's message. He tells Sue not to be late. What about this notice? (5. Schreiben Sie *tell* an.)

    S: They tell you not to smoke.
        usw.
        (6, 7, 8)

Weitere Schülerantworten:
6. They tell you not to drink this water.
7. They warn you not to swim near the rocks.
8. They warn people not to drive fast.

    L: (deuten Sie auf 5) This one means they don't allow you to smoke, doesn't it? And this one? (9. Schreiben Sie *allow* an.)

    S: They don't allow you to take dogs into the park.
        usw.
        (10, 11, 12 *School starts…*)

Weitere Schülerantworten:
10. They don't want you/people to take photos.
11. They don't want you to talk.
12. They don't expect you to be late.

IV Produzieren

Schilder und Notizen erklären
In Gruppen- oder Partnerarbeit werden die Schilder und Notizen schriftlich erklärt.

    L: Write down what all these notices and messages mean. Sometimes you can only write one sentence, but sometimes you can write two.

Als Hilfestellung können die Satzmuster A, B und C dienen, die Sie während der Phase I angeschrieben haben.

V Bewußtmachung

Look at this sentence:

Aunt Mary wants Bob to meet her.

When we use verbs like **want, tell, ask** and all the others we used today we need an object, like »Bob« and the infinitive with »to« of the verb.

		object	infinitive
Aunt Mary	**wants**	Bob	**to** meet her.

Lassen Sie weitere Beispiele aus der vorausgegangenen Lektion in die Tabelle eintragen.

Object + infinitive without »to« after certain verbs: see, hear, let, make s.o. do sth.

Policeman:	Now what can you tell me about the robbery?
Young woman:	I was outside the hairdresser's with my daughter. I noticed a car stop in front of the bank.
Man:	I saw two men get out.
Older woman:	I heard someone shout, »Help! Stop them!«
Young woman:	I saw the two men get into the car.
Man:	I watched the car turn left round the corner.
Young woman:	I made my daughter go into the hairdresser's to phone the police. Then I went into the bank.
Hairdresser:	Yes, I let the girl use my phone. I didn't see anything, but I heard the car drive away.
Girl:	I saw it drive away, too. I wrote the number down. The driver was a woman. She was about twenty with long, dark hair.
Policeman:	Well, that should help us a lot. Thank you very much.

I Demonstration

Das Thema *witnesses* kann durch ein kurzes Gespräch über die Beobachtungsgabe der Lernenden eingeführt werden.

L: Has anyone ever seen an accident or a robbery? If you did could you describe it? If you walk past someone in the street can you describe them afterwards? (Geben Sie den Lernenden Gelegenheit, kurz darauf zu antworten.)

129

Legen Sie die Folie auf den Tageslichtprojektor.

L: Look. There has been a bank robbery. All these people were in the street, so a policeman is talking to them. He wants to know what they saw. Listen to what they tell him.

Lesen Sie die Aussagen vor. Verändern Sie dabei Ihre Stimme, um zu zeigen, wer gerade spricht.

L: This young woman (Frau rechts) says, »I was outside the hairdresser's with my daughter. I noticed a car stop in front of the bank.«
This man says, »I saw two men get out.«
usw.

II Verstehen und Reagieren

Gedächtnisspiel: Falschaussagen
Bei zugedeckter Folie wiederholen Sie die Zeugenaussagen, wobei Sie absichtlich Falschaussagen machen. Aus dem Gedächtnis korrigieren die Schüler Ihre Aussagen, ohne jedoch die neue Struktur zu verwenden.

L: Now let's see how good you are at remembering things.

Decken Sie die Folie zu.

L: Listen again to what the young woman said. She told the policeman, »I noticed a car stop opposite the bank«. Is that right?
S1: No. In front of the bank.
L: Yes, you're right. She said, »I noticed a car stop in front of the bank«, didn't she?
Listen again: The man said, »I saw three men get out«. Is that right?
S2: No. Two men.
L: Yes, he said, »I saw two men get out«, didn't he?
usw.

Weitere Falschaussagen:
I heard someone shout, »Help! A robbery!«
I saw the men run away.
I watched the car turn right round the corner.
I made my daughter go into the café to phone the police.
I let the woman use my phone.
The hairdresser heard someone shout, »Help!«

III Reproduzieren

Rollenspiel
Die Szene wird mit verteilten Rollen gespielt. Dabei wird die Folie aufgedeckt, damit die Schüler die Sätze ablesen können. Übernehmen Sie selbst die Rolle der jungen Frau, um das neue Sprachmuster vorgeben zu können.

L: Let's act this scene. I'll be the young woman. Who wants to be the policeman, the man…?
All right. Let's start.

S1: Now what can you tell me about the robbery?

L: I was outside the hairdresser's with my daughter. I noticed a car stop in front of the bank.

S2: I saw…
usw.

IV Produzieren

Rollenspiel
Die gleiche Szene wird nun ohne Ihre Hilfe und mit zugedeckter Folie gespielt.

L: I'm going to cover the transparency up now. Let's see if you can do it again without any help. Who wants to be the policeman?
usw.

V Bewußtmachung

Schreiben Sie die folgenden Sätze an und erklären Sie die Struktur.

I	**noticed**	a car	**stop.**
	saw	two men	**get out.**
	. . .	. . .	. . .

Verbs like <u>notice, see, hear</u> and <u>watch</u> describe our <u>senses</u>. Another verb which describes our senses is <u>to feel</u>. After verbs like this we often use the infinitive, but we leave the »to« out. (Tragen Sie <u>senses</u> und »~~to~~« <u>infinitive</u> oberhalb der entsprechenden Spalten ein.)
We also need the infinitive without »to« after the verbs <u>let</u> and <u>make</u>.
Lassen Sie die Schüler weitere Beispiele aus der vorausgegangenen Lektion in die Tabelle eintragen.

Note:
Object + infinitive without »to« **or** Object + -ing form?

The infinitive is used if we see or hear the <u>whole</u> of the action, from beginning to end.
If we only see or hear part of it we use the **-ing form.**

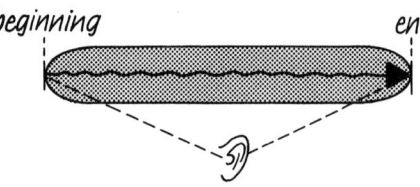

I heard Ann *play* a Beethoven Sonata. (= I heard *all* of it.)

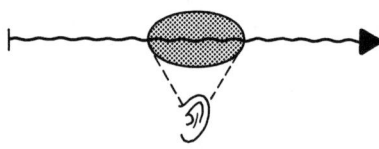

I heard Ann **playing** a Beethoven Sonata when I passed her house. (= I only heard **part** of it.)

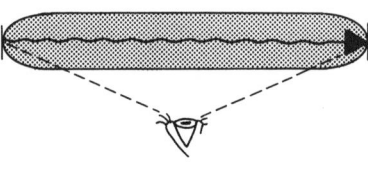

I saw a car *drive* down the street. (= I watched it the *whole* time.)

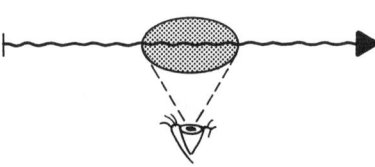

I saw a car **driving** down the street. (= I did not watch it all the time.)

Object + -ing form after verbs of perception:
he saw a man flying

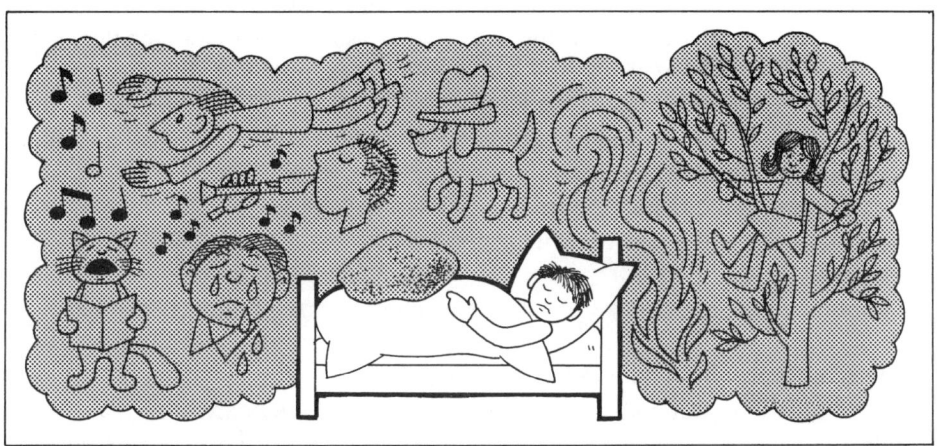

I Demonstration

Führen Sie das Thema mit einem kurzen Gespräch über Träume ein.

L: I had a marvellous/bad dream last night. Someone came to my house and said I could have three wishes – anything I wanted/Someone broke into my house…

Do you have dreams? Are they usually good ones or bad ones? Are they sometimes strange?

usw.

Legen Sie die Folie auf den Tageslichtprojektor und beschreiben Sie das Bild.

L: This is a boy called Chris. Last night he had a strange dream.

He saw a man flying.

He saw a dog wearing a hat.

He saw a girl sitting in a tree.

He heard a cat singing.

He heard a boy crying.

He heard someone playing the flute.

He smelt something burning.

He felt something lying on his bed.

II Verstehen und Reagieren

Anweisungen befolgen
In Anlehnung an die Folie zeichnen Sie nun ein Mädchen, das schläft. Dessen Träume werden von den Schülern nach Ihren Anweisungen bildhaft dargestellt. Benutzen Sie die gleichen Strukturen wie in der Phase I. Die handelnden Personen und Tiere können ausgetauscht bzw. durch andere bekannte Vokabeln ersetzt werden, z.B.

L: (Zeichnen Sie ein Mädchen, das schläft.) This is Eva. She had a strange dream last night, too.
She saw a cat flying. (Schreiben Sie den Satz an.)
Who can come and draw it?
usw.

Sie können einige Vorschläge für ganz einfache Strichzeichnungen machen.

Weitere mögliche Bestandteile des Traumes:
She saw a horse wearing trousers/a boy sitting on the cupboard/…
She heard a woman singing/a man laughing/someone playing the drums/…
She smelt something cooking
She felt someone lying on her bed/sitting on her feet/…

Schreiben Sie während der Traumbeschreibung weitere Beispiele für das neue Satzmuster an:
She heard a … …ing.
She smelt something cooking.
She felt something …ing…

III Reproduzieren

Rollenspiel
Beschreiben Sie jeweils einen Teil des Traumes von Chris unter Benutzung nur eines Verbs. Unter Verwendung desselben Verbs beschreiben die Lernenden den Traum von Eva.

L: Let's look at the differences between these two dreams. Chris saw a man flying. And Eva? She saw…? (Deuten Sie auf das entsprechende Satzmuster, das Sie während der Phase II angeschrieben haben.)
S1: She saw a horse wearing trousers.
L: Chris heard a cat singing. And Eva?
S2: She heard…
usw.

IV Produzieren

Rollenspiel
In der Rolle von Chris oder Eva erzählen die Schüler von »ihrem« Traum.
- L: Now (S1), let's say that you're Chris. Tell us about the dream you had last night.
- S1: I saw a man flying. I saw…
  usw.

Unter Verwendung der neuen Struktur können die Schüler dann einige Träume selbst erfinden und davon erzählen, z.B.
- S1: I saw a cow reading.
- S2: I heard…
  usw.

V Bewußtmachung

Erklären Sie die Struktur der folgenden Sätze:

Chris	saw	a man	flying.
	heard	a cat	singing.
	smelt	something	burning.
	felt		lying on his bed.

Verbs like <u>see, hear, smell</u> and <u>feel</u> describe our <u>senses</u>. After these verbs we often use the <u>-ing form.</u>
Lassen Sie die Schüler weitere Beispiele aus der vorausgegangenen Lektion finden.

Note:
Für den Vergleich mit der Struktur *object + infinitive without »to«* siehe **Object + infinitive without »to« after certain verbs.**

Passive: present perfect with and without »by-agent«

Um die Lernenden zu diesem frühen Zeitpunkt nicht zu überfordern, werden *by* + *agent* nur passiv und als unaufgeschlüsselte Vokabeln gelernt. Wenn Sie jedoch mehr Gewicht auf *by* + *agent* legen wollen, ändern Sie die Schlagzeilen, z.B. **New motorway opened by Princess Di, Man run over by bus, Paintings damaged by fire** usw.
In diesem Fall wird auch eine Regel für *by* + *agent* gegeben (V).

I Demonstration

Das Passiv mit dem *present perfect* wird anhand von Schlagzeilen aus britischen Zeitungen eingeführt. Bringen Sie eine britische Zeitung zur Illustration mit.
L: How many of you have ever seen a British newspaper? (Zeigen Sie auf einige Schlagzeilen in der mitgebrachten Zeitung und erklären Sie kurz eine oder zwei davon.) Look at these headlines. Can you understand them?
Decken Sie nun die folgenden Schlagzeilen auf (an der Tafel oder auf dem Tageslichtprojektor.)

New motorway opened	**150 teaching jobs lost**	**Painting sold for two million**
President not invited by Queen	**Five killed in fire**	**City Club closed by police**
Dog stolen from inside pop star's car	**Postwoman attacked by dog**	

L: What about these headlines? »New motorway opened« – that means a new motorway has been opened. (Schreiben Sie jeweils die Passivformen auf.) usw.
Die weiteren Schlagzeilen:
150 teaching jobs lost – 150 teaching jobs have been lost.
Painting sold for two million – A painting has been sold for two million.
President not invited by Queen – The President has not been invited by the Queen.
Five killed in fire – Five people have been killed in a fire.

136

City Club closed by police – The City Club/A club in the city <u>has been closed by</u> the police.

Dog stolen from inside pop star's car – A dog <u>has been stolen</u> from inside a pop star's car.

Postwoman attacked by dog – A postwoman <u>has been attacked by</u> a dog.

II Verstehen und Reagieren

Anweisungen befolgen: Hören und schreiben
Nach Ihren Anweisungen erstellen die Lernenden eigene Schlagzeilen, die an die Tafel bzw. auf den Tageslichtprojektor geschrieben werden.

L: Let's say you're all reporters and you have to write some reports. I'll tell you what's happened and you think of the headlines.
Listen: A sports centre has been opened by Princess Diana.
What's your headline?

S: Sports centre opened by Princess Diana.
usw.

Bei den weiteren Schlagzeilen können Sie Wortschatz und Wissen aus dem Unterricht mit einbeziehen.
Einige Vorschläge:
The new cinema has been closed – New cinema closed.
A missing boat has been found by children – Missing boat found by children.
Six people have been hurt in a car crash – Six hurt in car crash.
Nessie has been seen by fisherman – Nessie seen by fisherman.
A valuable painting has been stolen – Valuable painting stolen.
A castle has been sold to an American – Castle sold to American.
The South African team has not been invited to Britain – South African team/ South Africans not invited to Britain.
Protest letters have been sent to Downing Street – Protest letters sent to Downing Street /PM.

III Reproduzieren

Falschaussagen
Geben Sie absichtlich falsche Interpretationen für einige der in den Phasen I und II behandelten Schlagzeilen. Sie können z.B. die Verben verändern bzw. durch Hinzufügen von *not* oder *no* die Aussagen in ihr Gegenteil verkehren, z.B.:
New motorway opened – The new motorway <u>hasn't</u> been opened yet.
150 teaching jobs lost – <u>No</u> teaching jobs have been lost.

Die Lernenden müssen Ihre falschen Aussagen korrigieren.

L: I've got a very good memory, you know. I can remember all the news from the last few weeks. For example, I remember that the new motorway hasn't been opened yet. That's right, isn't it? (Um Sprechimpulse zu geben, deuten Sie auf die Passivformen, die Sie während der Phase I aufgeschrieben haben.)

S: No. It <u>has</u> been opened.

L: Oh well, that's only one thing I got wrong. I remember everything else. For example, I know that <u>no</u> teaching jobs have been lost. That's right, isn't it?

S: No. 150 (teaching jobs) have been lost.

Weitere Vorschläge:

The President <u>has</u> been invited by the Queen. (No, he <u>hasn't</u> been invited.)

<u>No-one</u> has been <u>hurt</u> in the fire. (No, <u>five</u> people have been <u>killed</u>.)

The City Club <u>hasn't</u> been closed. (No, it <u>has</u> been closed – by the police.)

A pop star's <u>car</u> has been stolen. (No, a <u>dog</u> has been stolen from inside it.)

A sports centre has been <u>bought</u> by Princess Diana. (No, it has been <u>opened</u> by her.)

The new cinema has been <u>opened</u>. (No, it has been <u>closed</u>.)

Six people have been <u>killed</u> in a car crash. (No, they have (only) been <u>hurt</u>.)

The South African team <u>has</u> been invited to Britain. (No, they have<u>n't</u> been invited.)

IV Produzieren

Rollenspiel

In Partnerarbeit wird ein Interview zwischen einem Polizisten und einer adligen Dame geübt, in deren Haus gerade eingebrochen wurde. Ermutigen Sie die Lernenden zur Improvisation, indem Sie sich nach dem gewünschten Wortschatz fragen oder ihn suchen lassen.

Teilen Sie die Arbeitsblätter aus.

L: The police have just received a phone call from Lady Moneybags. Her house has just been broken into.
    You need a partner. One of you is Lady Moneybags. The other is a police officer who is interviewing Lady Moneybags.

Führen Sie das Gespräch mit einem Schüler vor:

L: (S), you're Lady Moneybags and I'm the police officer.
    »Tell me, Lady Moneybags, has anyone been hurt?«

S: No. There was...
    usw.

Police officer	Lady Moneybags
Tell me, Lady Moneybags, has anyone been hurt?	
	No. There was no-one at home.
Do you know what's been stolen?	
	Some/A… have/has been taken out of… (handbag, drawer, cupboard, pockets …).
Has anything been damaged?	
	Yes. The … (windows, door lock …) have/has been broken, knocked over, scratched, cut …).
Is there anything else you've noticed?	
	Yes. All the (drawers, cupboards …) have been emptied. (My clothes …) have been thrown on the floor.
Have any strangers been seen round here?	
	I haven't seen anyone/Yes, …
Now you are Lady Moneybags.	**Now you are the police officer.**

Nachdem die Paare einige Zeit geübt haben, führen sie ihre Dialoge der Klasse vor.

V Bewußtmachung

For things that <u>have happened</u> in the past – if we <u>do not know</u> who has done something or if it <u>does not matter</u> we use the passive, formed with the present perfect.

	has/have been + past participle	
A new motorway	**has been**	**opened**
Five people	**have been**	**killed**

By + agent
If it is <u>important</u> to know who did something we can use <u>by.</u> We call the person who did it the <u>agent.</u>

> The City Club has been closed **by the police.**
> The new motorway has been opened **by Princess Di.**

We use <u>by,</u> too, if the <u>agent</u> is <u>not a person</u>.

A man has been run over by a bus.
Some paintings have been damaged **by fire.**

Look at the differences between active and passive.

Active: The police have closed the City Club.
Passive: The City Club has been closed **by the police.**

If we want to show that the agent is very important (the police, not anyone else) we use the *by + agent* construction rather than an active sentence.

Passive: simple present

I Demonstration

Das Passiv wird anhand der folgenden neun Gegenstände eingeführt. Die Gegenstände können an die Tafel oder auf den Tageslichtprojektor skizziert werden. Sie können Fotos aus Zeitschriften ausschneiden oder, soweit wie möglich, Realgegenstände mitbringen. Die Gegenstände erscheinen in der vorgegebenen Reihenfolge.

Jaguar	Rolls	Mini
fork	knife	chair
sandwich	bread roll	loaf of bread

Bevor Sie die Zeichnungen zeigen, führen Sie das Thema »britische Autos« wie folgt ein.

L: How many of you are interested in cars? Do you know any British cars?
Decken Sie nun die Zeichnungen auf.

L: Look, here's a Jaguar. It's made in Britain. (Schreiben Sie *made in Britain* auf.) And here's a Rolls. That's made in Britain, too. And the Mini's made in Britain. All three cars are made in Britain. Now look at these objects. They're all made of different materials: the fork's made of plastic, the knife's made of metal and the chair? Do you know what it's made of – in English?

S: Wood.

L: That's right. The chair's made of wood.

usw.

In ähnlicher Weise führen Sie *used for eating* (knife, fork), *eaten with the fingers* (sandwich, roll) und *sold at the baker's* (roll, loaf) ein.

II Verstehen und Reagieren

Zuordnen
Den Lernenden werden nun weitere Bilder (Fotos, Realgegenstände) gezeigt, die sie verschiedenen Kategorien zuordnen müssen. Die Bilder können dem Wortschatz der Klasse angepaßt werden. Sie können die Aktivität auch als Wettbewerb mit Punkten für richtige Antworten durchführen. Die Anordnung der Gegenstände ist unwichtig.

Mercedes	rough wooden kitchen table	bread roll
sandals	thick woollen sweater	sheet of paper	sunglasses
pencil	woollen child's cap	loaf of bread
VW Golf	heavy winter boots	British sandwich

L: Now look at these pictures. We're going to play a game. Listen first. Don't write anything down yet. I want you to write down all the things that are made in Germany. (Schreiben Sie jeweils die Kategorie auf, z.B. <u>made in Germany</u>.)
And then write down everything that is <u>made of wood, made of wool</u>, everything that is <u>worn in winter, worn in summer</u> and <u>worn on the feet</u>. Then everything that is <u>used for writing, sold at the baker's, eaten with the fingers</u> and everything that is <u>found in the kitchen</u>.

Geben Sie nun der Klasse Zeit, um alleine, mit einem Partner oder in der Gruppe nach den Lösungen zu suchen.

III Reproduzieren

Zuordnen
Überprüfen Sie nun die Antworten. Wenn die Aktivität als Mannschaftswettbewerb durchgeführt wurde, achten Sie darauf, daß jeweils verschiedene Sprecher die Antworten vorlesen.

L: Now let's see if you've got it right.

Schreiben Sie folgenden Sprechimpuls auf: … are <u>made in Germany</u>.

S: Mercedes and Golf are made in Germany.
L: Has anybody got anything different? No? Well, you're right. What's next?
S: The table and the pencil are made of wood.
usw.

Lösungen:
made in Germany: Mercedes, Golf
made of wood: table, pencil
made of wool: sweater, cap
worn in winter: sweater, cap, boots
worn in summer: sandals, sunglasses

worn on the feet: sandals, boots
used for writing: paper, pencil
sold at the baker's: roll, loaf of bread
eaten with the fingers: roll, sandwich
found in the kitchen: table, roll, loaf of bread

IV Produzieren

Geheime Auswahl
Die Schüler denken sich entweder einen der abgebildeten oder einen anderen
Gegenstand aus, den sie mit Hilfe des Passivs beschreiben und der von den Mitschülern erraten wird. Schlagen Sie auch andere Verben vor, z.B. played (sports) by
(number of people, teams, men…), in (summer, Germany …); eaten at (time of
year or day), in, by (country); grown (food) in (country, part of country); bought,
used by (type, age of person); closed (type of shop, institution) on (day); done (type
of work) by (type of person); taught (school subject) by (woman, young person…)
usw.
Sie können die Schüler auch dazu ermutigen, ihre landeskundlichen Kenntnisse
einzusetzen, z.B. *They're found at the Tower of London* (Beefeaters); *They're sold at
British post offices* (postcards). Die Zahl der Fragen sollte beschränkt werden. Zunächst sollten allgemeinere Fragen vorgezogen werden, z.B. *Is it played in summer?
Is it a team game?* Spezifischere Fragen wie z.B. *Is it cricket?* sollten erst dann gestellt werden, wenn der Fragende sich ziemlich sicher ist. Die Aktivität kann auch
als Wettbewerb organisiert werden.

    L: I'm thinking of a sport. It's played in Britain. You can ask (six) questions.
    S: Is it a team game?
        usw.
Die Schüler übernehmen dann die Lehrerrolle.

V Bewußtmachung

If we do not know who does something or if it does not matter we use the passive.

is/are + past participle

Jaguars	**are**	**made** in Britain.
Bread	**is**	**sold** at the baker's.

Past continuous

I Demonstration

Gestern abend wurde im Jugendzentrum Marias Radio gestohlen. Die anwesenden Jugendlichen erklären, weshalb sie nicht der Dieb gewesen sein können. Zeigen Sie folgende Bilder.

> L: Last night at the youth club somebody took Maria's radio. She arrived at half past seven and put it on a table. But at a quarter to eight it wasn't there. She asked everybody about it. Dave and Janet told her, »We didn't take it. We were dancing.« Derek said, »I was reading a magazine.« (Schreiben Sie jeweils die »past continuous«-Form auf.)
> usw.

Linda and Paul – playing table tennis
Mario and Carla – making coffee
Pete and Sylvia – looking at photos
Ben and Anna – playing chess
Sue, Ron and Joe – talking

Bemerkung: Vermeiden Sie zu diesem Zeitpunkt die Frageform »*What were you doing?*«, da sie die Lernenden häufig zu der grammatisch falschen Antwort* »I was **doing** reading« verleitet.

144

II Verstehen und Reagieren

Geheime Auswahl
Anhand Ihrer Beschreibungen versuchen die Schüler zu erraten, an welche der ab-gebildeten Personen Sie gerade denken.

L: I wonder who took Maria's radio. I know one person who didn't. He was reading. Do you know who I mean?

S: Derek.

L: Yes. Derek was reading a magazine, wasn't he? And two people were playing chess.

S: Ben and Anna.

L: That's right. Ben and Anna were playing chess. So it wasn't them. Some other people were looking at photos.

usw.

III Reproduzieren

Gedächtnisspiel: Falschaussagen
Nachdem sich die Lernenden die Bilder eingeprägt haben, decken Sie sie zu. Durch bewußt falsche Aussagen prüfen Sie ihre Gedächtnisleistungen nach. Diese Aktivität kann auch als Wettbewerb zwischen Einzelschülern oder Gruppen durchgeführt werden.

L: Can you remember what everybody was doing between half past seven and a quarter to eight? Look at the pictures and try to remember them. But don't write anything down. (Decken Sie die Bilder nach einigen Minuten zu.) Now what about Ben? He was dancing, wasn't he?

S: No, he was playing chess.

L: That's right. Ben was playing chess. (One point for you/your team.) And Sylvia? She was making coffee, wasn't she?

usw.

Bei falschen Schülerantworten können Sie die Bilder kurz aufdecken.

IV Produzieren

Auskunft erbitten und erteilen
In Gruppen spielen die Schüler eine ähnliche Szene. Eine Person ist Maria, die nach ihrem Radio fragt, die anderen sind Mitglieder des Jugendzentrums, die Maria verdächtigt. Da diese Schüler sich selbst spielen, sollten sie dazu ermutigt werden, auch andere Tätigkeiten als die in dem Demonstrationsschritt genannten anzuführen.

L: One of you is Maria. Ask the others about your radio.
Schreiben Sie die erste Frage und die Antwortstruktur auf:

> - Do you know anything about my radio?
> - No, I was …ing.
>   Yes, …

Die Rolle von Maria wird ein paarmal gewechselt.

V Bewußtmachung

For something that <u>was going on</u> at a certain time in the past we use the <u>past continuous</u>.

> Between half past seven and a quarter to eight Linda and Paul **were** play**ing** table tennis. Derek **was** read**ing**.

We often use the past continuous together with the simple past: the past continuous shows that a <u>longer</u> action or situation was going on when something interrupted it.

Past perfect

I Demonstration

Legen Sie den Lernenden die folgende Folie bzw. das folgende Arbeitsblatt vor:

L: Yesterday was Bill's birthday. He had planned to give himself a present of a great evening out – first a disco, then the theatre. Look what happened. (Lesen Sie die Sätze vor.)

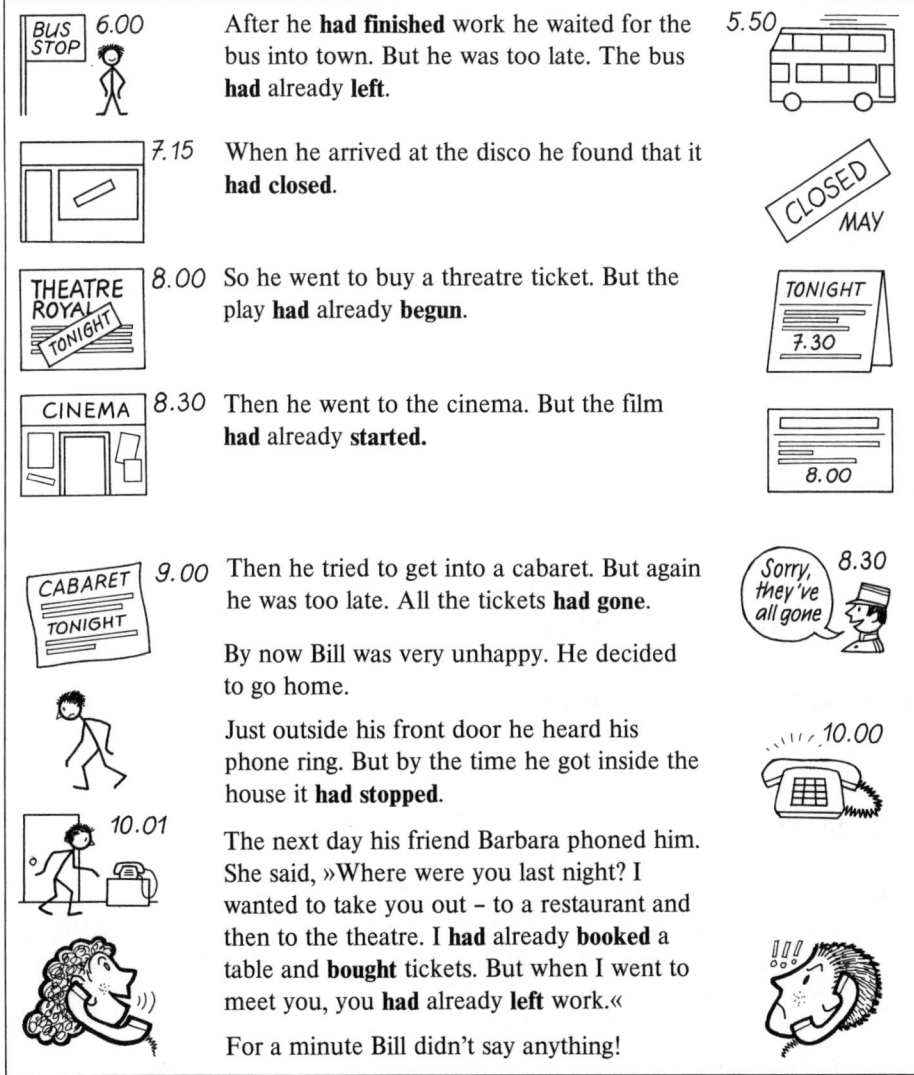

After he **had finished** work he waited for the bus into town. But he was too late. The bus **had** already **left**.

When he arrived at the disco he found that it **had closed**.

So he went to buy a threatre ticket. But the play **had** already **begun**.

Then he went to the cinema. But the film **had** already **started.**

Then he tried to get into a cabaret. But again he was too late. All the tickets **had gone**.

By now Bill was very unhappy. He decided to go home.

Just outside his front door he heard his phone ring. But by the time he got inside the house it **had stopped**.

The next day his friend Barbara phoned him. She said, »Where were you last night? I wanted to take you out – to a restaurant and then to the theatre. I **had** already **booked** a table and **bought** tickets. But when I went to meet you, you **had** already **left** work.«

For a minute Bill didn't say anything!

II Verstehen und Reagieren

Zuordnen: Hören und schreiben
Schreiben Sie die Sätze der folgenden Tabelle an die Tafel oder auf den Tageslicht-projektor und lesen Sie sie vor. Die erste Folie wird zugedeckt. Die Lernenden ent-scheiden, welches Ereignis als erstes passierte, und tragen dann den entsprechen-den Buchstaben ein. Um die Aufgaben zu erleichtern, können Sie die erste Folie aufdecken und auf die Uhrzeiten hinweisen.

L: Bill had a terrible birthday, didn't he? Listen again to everything that happened. Think about what happened first.
   A: »After he had finished work« or B: »He waited for the bus into town.«
S: A was first.
   usw.

A	B	A/B
1 After he had finished work	he waited for the bus into town.	
2 He waited for the bus,	but the bus had already left.	
3 He arrived at the disco,	but it had closed.	
4 The play had already begun	when he went to buy a theatre ticket.	
5 When he got to the cinema	the film had already started.	
6 All the tickets had gone	when he tried to get into a cabaret.	
7 The phone had stopped	by the time he got inside the house.	
8 When Barbara went to meet Bill	he had already left work.	

Lösungen: 1A, 2B, 3B, 4A, 5B, 6A, 7A, 8B

III Reproduzieren

Zuordnen
Legen Sie der Klasse folgendes Arbeitsblatt vor oder schreiben Sie die Sätze auf. Arbeiten Sie die Aufgaben mündlich durch:

L: Look at these sentences (1):
   »The film started. Then Bill arrived at the cinema.«
   What happened first?

S: The film started.

L: That's right. Now look at the next two sentences. (Lesen Sie die beiden Sätze unter 1 vor.) Which is correct?

S: The film had already started when Bill arrived at the cinema.

L: Yes. Now look at number two. Usw.

---

1. The film started. Then Bill arrived at the cinema.
   The film had already started when Bill arrived at the cinema.
   Bill had already arrived at the cinema when the film started.

2. The phone stopped. Then Bill opened the door.
   When the phone stopped Bill had already opened the door.
   When Bill opened the door the phone had already stopped.

3. The police arrived. Then the burglar escaped.
   When the police arrived the burglar had already escaped.
   The police had already arrived when the burglar escaped.

4. Pete found a job. Then he left school.
   When Pete found a job he had already left school.
   When Pete left school he had already found a job.

5. Tony did his homework. Then he read some comics.
   After Tony had read some comics he did his homework.
   After Tony had done his homework he read some comics.

6. I finished my book. Then I went to bed.
   I had already finished my book when I went to bed.
   I went to bed before I had finished my book.

7. Maria went out at seven. I phoned her about eight.
   I phoned Maria, but she had already gone out.
   After I had phoned Maria she went out.

8. Mrs Kelly sold her car. Then she bought a bike.
   After Mrs Kelly had bought a bike she sold her car.
   After Mrs Kelly had sold her car she bought a bike.

9. Anna started English and then went to London for a year.
   When Anna went to London she had already started English.
   When Anna started English she had already gone to London.

Lösungen:
1. The film had already started when Bill arrived at the cinema.
2. When Bill opened the door the phone had already stopped.
3. The police had already arrived when the burglar escaped.
4. When Pete left school he had already found a job.
5. After Tony had done his homework he read some comics.
6. I had already finished my book when I went to bed.
7. I phoned Maria, but she had already gone out.
8. After Mrs Kelly had sold her car she bought a bike.
9. When Anna went to London she had already started English.

IV Produzieren

Lückentext

Die Sätze auf der Bildfolie werden zugedeckt, so daß nur beide Bildreihen sichtbar sind. In Gruppen- oder Partnerarbeit versuchen die Schüler, die Bildgeschichte in Phase I selbst zu erzählen. Je nach Leistungsstand der Klasse kann einiges angegeben werden, wie z.B. im folgenden Lückentext.

After Bill had.................. work he.................................	finished
into town. But... The bus.........	waited for
already...........................	too late
	left
When he........................... disco it..............................	closed
So he went... But the play	buy
....	begun
Then.. But the film...........	started
....	
Then he tried...................... a....................... But again	get into
he was....................... All the tickets..........................	
By now Bill was........................ He decided to.................	
Just outside his........................... he heard....................	inside
ring. But by the time he................................. the house it	stopped
....	

150

The next day... She phoned
said, »... I wanted to booked
.... – to..................... and then to..............
I .... a table and.....................
tickets. But when I went to meet you, you ....
work.«

For a minute........ didn't...........................!

Die Sätze auf der Bildfolie werden anschließend aufgedeckt und mit den Schülerantworten verglichen.

V Bewußtmachung

When we think of a <u>certain time in the past</u> and want to talk about something that
happened <u>before</u> that time we use the past perfect for the thing that happened first.

When Bill went to the cinema	the film **had** already **started**.
certain time in past	this happened before
After Sue **had read** some comics	she did her homework.
this happened before	certain time in past

Present continuous: affirmative

Legen Sie die folgende Folie auf den Tageslichtprojektor.

She/he is/they are …ing

I Demonstration

Lehrerfragen wie *What is (she) doing?* müssen bei der ersten Einführung der »-ing Form« vermieden werden, um nicht falsche Schülerantworten wie z.B.* *She is doing reading* zu provozieren.
Beschreiben Sie die Abbildungen wie folgt.

    L: Look at all these people. (Deuten Sie auf die jeweilige Abbildung.) Sue is watching TV, John is reading a book…
        usw.

Lösungen:
Sue – watching TV, John – reading a book, Linda – eating chips, Tony and Janet – playing cards, Ann – eating an ice-cream, Marie – riding a bike, Mike – listening to music/the radio, Alan – reading a magazine, Joe and Barbara – playing table tennis, Dave and Carol – talking

II Verstehen und Reagieren

Geheime Auswahl
Denken Sie an eine der abgebildeten Personen und beschreiben Sie sie. Die Schüler sollen sie erraten.

    L: Now listen: He is listening to the radio. Who is it?
    S: Mike.
    L: That's right. Let's try again: They are talking.
    S: Carol and Dave.
        usw.

III Reproduzieren

Gedächtnisspiel: Falschaussagen
Decken Sie die Bilder zu und machen Sie absichtlich falsche Aussagen über die Personen. Die Schüler korrigieren Ihre Aussagen.

    L: Now let's see what you can remember. Is this right or wrong?
        Sue is reading a book.
  S1: Wrong. She is watching TV.
  S2: That's right.
        (Lassen Sie einige Schüler dazu Stellung nehmen.)
    L: Sue is watching TV.
        Listen again: Carol and Dave are talking. Is that right or wrong?
  S1: That's right.
        usw.

Wenn sich die Schüler nur noch unklar an die Bilder erinnern können, werden die Abbildungen kurz aufgedeckt. Danach kann das Frage-Antwort-Spiel bei zugedeckten Bildern wiederaufgenommen werden.

IV Produzieren

Gedächtnisspiel
Die Bilder werden abgedeckt.

    L: Now let's see what you can remember. What can you tell me about all these people? Marie…? John is…?
  S1: John is reading a magazine.
    L: Is that right?
  S2: No, he is reading a book.
    L: That's right. And?
  S3: Sue is watching TV.
        usw.

Bei Unklarheiten werden die verschiedenen Schülervorschläge notiert und später mit den Abbildungen verglichen. Es können Punkte für richtige Antworten vergeben werden, z.B. bei einem Mannschaftswettbewerb.

I am/you are …ing

I Demonstration

Stellen Sie einige in den Bildern dargestellte Tätigkeiten pantomimisch dar.
    L: Look, I am (riding a bike).
         Now I am (playing table tennis).
         usw.

Da der Transfer von der 3. Person Sing. zur 1. und 2. Person Sing. im allgemeinen keine Schwierigkeit bereitet, kann der zweite Schritt »Verstehen und Reagieren« entfallen.

III Reproduzieren

Falschaussagen
Ein Schüler stellt eine der abgebildeten Tätigkeiten pantomimisch vor der ganzen Klasse dar. Erraten Sie diese Tätigkeit absichtlich falsch und bitten Sie dann die Klasse um weitere Deutungsvorschläge.
    S1: (Mimt)
    L: You are playing table tennis.
    S1: No.
    L: Then I don't know. Can you help me?
    S2: You are …
        usw.
Weitere in den Bildern nicht vorkommende Tätigkeiten können eingeführt werden, z.B. *cleaning shoes/teeth/the board/a window, dancing, doing homework, knitting, writing a letter/on the board …*

IV Produzieren

Geheime Auswahl
Das Ratespiel unter III wird ohne die Vermittlung der Lehrkraft zwischen Einzelschülern und Klasse weitergeführt.

S1: (Mimt)
S2: You are cleaning your shoes.
S1: That's right.
    usw.

V Bewußtmachung

We use the <u>present continuous</u> when people are doing things **now,** while we are talking.

John **is** read**ing** a book.
Tony and Janet **are** play**ing** cards. } **Now**

Present continuous: interrogative:
is she/he ... ing?

Legen Sie die folgende Folie auf den Tageslichtprojektor.

I Demonstration

Lehrerfragen wie *What is (she) doing?* müssen bei der ersten Einführung der
»-ing Form« vermieden werden, um nicht falsche Schülerantworten wie z.B.* *She
is doing reading* zu provozieren.
Machen Sie Deutungsvorschläge für jedes Bild. In dieser Phase hören die Lernenden nur zu.

L: Look at Martin. Is he riding a bike? Or is he playing the piano? Is he riding a
horse? Maybe.
And Marie. Is she riding a bike?
usw.

Deutungsvorschläge:
Martin – riding a bike, Marie – riding a horse, Sue – reading, Don – writing, Karen –
playing the piano, Tony – playing tennis, Lynne – driving a car, Eric – watching TV,
Jackie – skiing, Mike – playing football, Barbara – typing, Paul – swimming

II Verstehen und Reagieren

Bilder interpretieren
    L: Look at Martin. Is he riding a horse?
    S1: No. He is riding a bike.
    L: Who thinks (S1) is right? Put your hands up. And the others?
    S2: He is playing the piano.
    L: Who thinks that's right? Put your hands up – I see, most of you think he is riding a bike.
        Now look at Marie. Is she…?
        usw.

III Reproduzieren

Bilder interpretieren
Machen Sie für jedes Bild einige Deutungsvorschläge. Ein Schüler sucht einen dieser Vorschläge aus oder macht einen eigenen und bittet dann die Mitschüler um ihre Meinungen.
    L: Look at Martin. Is he riding a horse? Is he riding a bike? Or is he playing the piano? (S1), ask the class.
    S1: Is he riding a bike?
    S2: Yes.
    L: Who thinks that's right? Put your hands up.
        Now let's look at Marie. Is she riding a bike? Is she writing? (S2), ask the class.
    S2: Is she (riding a horse)?
        usw.

IV Produzieren

Geheime Auswahl
Jeweils zwei Schüler stehen vor der Klasse. Schüler 1 stellt eine der abgebildeten Tätigkeiten pantomimisch dar, Schüler 2 beantwortet Deutungsvorschläge aus der Klasse.
    L: Now I want two people to come out here. (S1), you do one of these things (zeigt auf die Abbildungen) – or something else, if you like. (Weitere Tätigkeiten werden aufgeschrieben, z.B. *play (sports, musical instruments), skate, write letters/on the board…*). Tell your partner what you are doing, but don't tell the others. The rest of you ask (S2): Is he reading? Is he writing a letter? and so on.

S3: Is he reading?
S2: No.
S4: Is he...?
     usw.

V Bewußtmachung

We use the present continuous to ask what people are doing **now,** while we are talking.

> **Is** Martin rid**ing** a horse?
> **Is** Marie writ**ing**?

Present perfect: affirmative: Anna has got up
negative: Mike has not got up yet

Legen Sie folgende Folie auf den Tageslichtprojektor.

Munich   **Manchester**

get up?

Anna has already got up.
Mike has not got up yet.

have breakfast?

Anna has already had breakfast.
Mike has not had breakfast yet.

leave the house?

Anna has already left the house.
Mike has not left the house yet.

start work?

Anna has already started work.
Mike has not started work yet.

do the shopping?

Anna has already done the shopping.
Mike has not done the shopping yet.

go home?

Anna has already gone home.
Mike has not gone home yet.

have tea?

Anna has already had her tea.
Mike has not had his tea yet.

try to ring?

Anna has already tried to ring Mike.
Mike has not come home yet.

have lunch?

Anna has already had lunch.
Mike has not had lunch yet.

read the paper?

Anna has already read the paper.
Mike has not read the paper yet.

finish work?

Anna has already finished work.
Mike has not finished work yet.

go to bed?

Mike has tried to ring Anna.
But Anna has already gone to bed.

I Demonstration

Besprechen Sie die Bildpaare unter Verwendung der jeweiligen Satzpaare.

L: Look at these pictures. On the left there's Anna. She lives in Munich. She has an English friend called Mike. He lives in Manchester. This is what happens on one day. Look at the differences between Anna and Mike. (Deuten Sie auf das erste Bildpaar): Anna has already got up. Mike has not got up yet.
usw.

II Verstehen und Reagieren

Hörverstehen: Zuordnen
Machen Sie sich eine Schablone, mit der Sie die Satzpaare zudecken können. Die Lernenden versuchen das Bild zu identifizieren, das Sie beschreiben.

L (bei zugedeckten Sätzen): Anna has started work. Which picture is that? Come and show me.
S: (Zeigt auf das betreffende Bild.)

Verwenden Sie bei Ihren Beschreibungen Negativsätze nicht nur für Mike, sondern auch für Anna, z.B.

L: Anna has <u>not</u> done the shopping <u>yet</u>. (Bild: *finish work?*)

Wenn Sie im Zusammenhang mit Mike Affirmativsätze verwenden, muß *already* jedoch wegfallen.

   L: Mike <u>has</u> had breakfast. (Bild: *leave the house?*)

III Reproduzieren

Kettenbilden
Teilen Sie folgendes Arbeitsblatt aus oder schreiben Sie die Sätze auf eine Folie.

---

  1. Sue does not go to school any more. – She has left school.
     Colin does not work at the bank any more. He ....
  2. Joe: »I'm hungry. What's for lunch?« – Joe has not had any lunch yet.
     Barbara: »I'm hungry. Is tea ready?« – Barbara ....
  3. Robert: »That's the end of work for today.« – Robert has finished work.
     Helen: »No more homework now.« – Helen ....
  4. Graham goes to school now. – He has started school.
     Cathy has got her first job. She ....
  5. Barry is still at university. – He has not left university yet.
     Angela still goes to school. – She ....
  6. Pat is not in. – She has gone out.
     Simon is not in. He is at the youth club. – He ....
  7. Martin's first driving lesson is next week. – He has not started his driving lessons yet.
     Marie is going to do her homework in a minute. – She ....
  8. Stuart knows what is in the newspaper. – He has read the paper.
     Sandra knows what the book is about. – She ....
  9. Oliver will give you your book back tomorrow. – He has not finished it yet.
     Christine is writing a letter to her pen-friend. – She ....
 10. Pete is going to read the paper now. – He has not read the paper yet.
     Jane would like to read the comic. – She ....
 11. Mark has no more shopping to do. – He has done the shopping.
     Gina has no more homework to do. – She ....

Geben Sie für jedes Satzpaar das Muster vor.

    L: Look at the first two sentences: Sue does not go to school any more. She has left school.
         And Colin?
  S1: He has left the bank.
    L: Joe has not had any lunch yet. And Barbara?
  S2: She has not had any tea yet.
         usw.

Lösungen:
3. Helen has finished her homework.
4. Cathy has started work/her first job.
5. Angela has not left school yet.
6. Simon has gone to the youth club.
7. Marie has not started her homework yet.
8. Sandra has read the book.
9. Christine has not finished the letter/it yet.
10. Jane has not read the comic yet.
11. Gina has done her homework.

IV Produzieren

Bilder beschreiben
Legen Sie die Schablone auf die Folie, so daß die Sätze zugedeckt sind. Die Lernenden beschreiben die Bilder ohne Ihre Hilfe.

L: Now let's see what you've learnt today. Can you talk about these pictures? Start with the first one. Anna has…?

S1: Anna has already got up.
(Deuten Sie auf die jeweiligen Bilder.)

S2: Mike has not got up yet.

S3: Anna has…
usw.

V Bewußtmachung

L: Look at these sentences.

Anna has finished work.	Mike has not got up yet.
I have seen that film.	The film has not started yet.
Someone has eaten my sweets.	I have not done my homework.

In these sentences (deuten Sie auf die Affirmativsätze, links) someone has done something.

In these sentences (die Negativsätze) someone has not done something.

We are mostly interested in the fact that someone has or has not done something – in the results or consequences for the present or future.

162

Anna can go home now.	Mike is still in bed.
I know what the film is about.	We will see the beginning.
They are all gone.	There will be trouble.

To show that we are mostly interested in the <u>results</u> or <u>consequences</u> we use the <u>present perfect.</u>

To form the present perfect we need the verb »to have« plus the <u>past participle</u> of the verb you need in order to talk about what has happened:

to have + past participles   (Tafelanschrieb)

These, for instance, are past participles: got up, had, left.

Can you find some more?

Weitere Beispiele von der Folie: started, finished, done, gone, tried, come, read.

L: Now, so that you don't have to learn each one of these past participles there is a rule.

To form the past participles of some verbs you just add »-ed« to the infinitive. These are called <u>regular verbs:</u> start – start<u>ed</u>, finish – finish<u>ed</u>, try – tri<u>ed</u> (y → i), comb – comb<u>ed</u>.

Other verbs are called <u>irregular</u> ones and you have to learn all their past participles separately: get – <u>got</u>, have – <u>had</u>.

Here are the infinitives of some irregular verbs. Try to find their past participles from the transparency: leave, do, go, come, read. (Partner- oder Gruppenarbeit)

Lösungen: left, done, gone, come, read.

Present perfect: interrogative: have we/you; has she/he...?

Legen Sie folgende Folie auf den Tageslichtprojektor.

Paul

Liz

Checklist

– change money *(all)*
– collect tickets *(Liz)*
– pack radio *(Maria)*
– do all the shopping *(all)*
– buy the presents *(all)*
– tell postman *(Liz)*
– give address to neighbours *(Johnny)*
– ask neighbours to feed budgie *(Maria)*
– take dog to Johnny's father *(Liz)*
– water plants

Johnny

Maria

I Demonstration

Formen Sie die Notizen der obigen Checkliste zur Ferienplanung in *present perfect*-Fragen um und schreiben Sie bei jedem Satz die Partizipien auf.

L: These four young people want to go on holiday together. They are going to see some friends in England. Paul and Liz are checking that they have done everything.
(Deuten Sie auf die jeweilige Zeile der Checkliste.)
Paul asks Liz, »Have we changed money?« (Schreiben Sie *changed* auf.)
»Have you collected the tickets, Liz?«
»Has Maria packed the radio?«
»Have we done all the shopping?«
»Have we bought the presents?«
»Have you told the postman, Liz?«
»Has Johnny given our address to the neighbours?«

»Has Maria asked the neighbours to feed the budgie?«
»Have you taken the dog to Johnny's father, Liz?«
»Has someone watered the plants?«

II Verstehen und Reagieren

Information erfragen und erteilen
Legen Sie eine zweite Folie über die Checkliste. Auf der zweiten Folie sind folgende Stichpunkte abgehakt: *change money, collect tickets, do all the shopping, buy the presents, give address to neighbours.*

    L: Have they done all these things? Let's see.
         (Deuten Sie auf die jeweiligen Stichpunkte.)
         Have they changed money?
  S1: Yes, (they have).
    L: Has Liz collected the tickets?
  S2: Yes, (she has).
    L: Has Maria packed the radio?
  S3: No, (she hasn't).
    L: No, not yet.
         usw.

Weitere Fragen:
Have they done all the shopping? (Yes)
Have they bought the presents? (Yes)
Has Liz told the postman? (No, not yet)
Has Johnny given the address to the neighbours? (Yes)
Has Maria asked the neighbours to feed the budgie? (No, not yet)
Has Liz taken the dog to Johnny's father? (No, not yet)
Has anyone watered the plants? (No, not yet)

III Reproduzieren

Information erfragen und erteilen
Legen Sie eine dritte Folie auf den Tageslichtprojektor oder schreiben Sie sie an die Tafel.

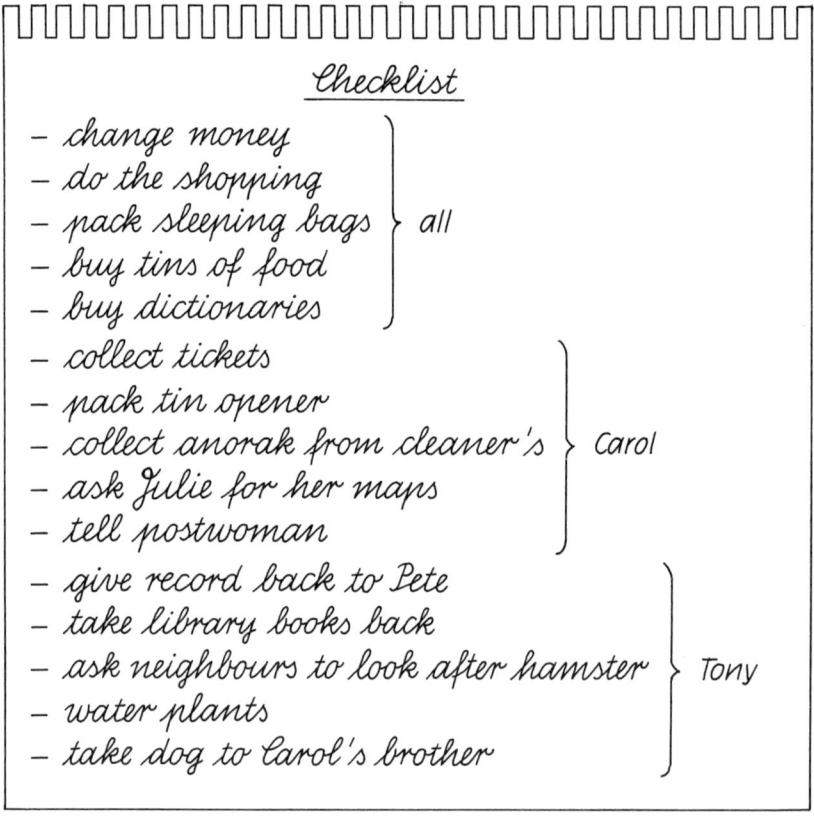

Ein Schüler (S1) bekommt die gleiche Liste, auf der aber folgende Stichworte abgehakt sind: *change money, pack sleeping bags, buy tins of food, collect tickets, ask Julie for her maps, give record back to Pete, ask neighbours to look after hamster.* Die Lernenden erkundigen sich bei S1 nach den Tätigkeiten, die schon verrichtet sind, und nach denen, die noch bevorstehen. Jede schon verrichtete Tätigkeit wird auf der Folie bzw. an der Tafel abgehakt. Geben Sie bei den Stichworten *change money, collect tickets* und *give record back zu Pete* das jeweilige Muster vor: *Have they/she/he...?*

L: I want someone to come out here. (Geben Sie diesem Schüler, S1, die Liste mit den abgehakten Stichworten.)

Tony, Helen and Carol are going camping in Scotland. But there are a lot of things to do before they can leave.

Have they changed money?

S1: Yes, (they have).

L: So you can tick that off. (S1 hakt diese Tätigkeit auch auf der Folie bzw. an der Tafel ab.)

(Wenden Sie sich an die Klasse): Now **you** ask, »Have they...?«

S2: Have they done the shopping? (Als Hilfestellung weisen Sie auf die Partizipien, die Sie während der Phase I angeschrieben haben.)

usw.

L: And what about Carol? Has she done everything? Has she collected the tickets?

usw.

IV Produzieren

Information erfragen und erteilen

Das Gespräch unter III wird nun in Partnerarbeit geübt. Teilen Sie folgende zwei Arbeitsblätter an die Schülerpaare aus.

Partner A	Partner B
You, your partner and two friends, Frank and Sylvia, are going to see your English penfriends.	You, your partner and two friends, Frank and Sylvia, are going to see your English penfriends.
1. Has your partner done all these things? Ask:	1. Your partner is going to ask you some questions. Answer them like this:
Have you...? (taken, bought, packed) - take your library books back - buy a present for your penfriend - pack your radio	- Yes, I have. - No, I haven't. - No, not yet.
2. Now your partner is going to ask you some questions. Answer them like this: - Yes, he has. - No, he hasn't. - No, not yet.	2. Has Frank done all these things? Ask: Has Frank...? (done, collected, packed) - do the shopping

- collect the tickets
- pack his bag

3. Has Sylvia done all these things?
Ask your partner:
Has Sylvia...? (changed, asked)
- buy a tin opener
- change her money
- ask her sister for maps

3. Answer your partner's questions now.

4. Now answer your partner's questions.

4. There are some things that Frank and Sylvia are going to do together.
Ask your partner:
Have they...? (changed, bought)
- change their money
- buy dictionaries
- do their shopping

Zur weiteren Übung können Partner A und B ihre Arbeitsblätter gegenseitig austauschen.

V Bewußtmachung

L: Sometimes we ask about things that have already happened – or things that have not happened yet. We ask about things that are past, but are still important for the present or future. For example,
    Have you packed your radio? = Is it in the bag **now**?
    Has Carol collected the tickets? = **Will** we be able to get on the boat?

For questions like this we need the present perfect:

to have	+	past participle
Have they		bought dictionaries?
Has Frank		done the shopping?
. . .		. . .

Lassen Sie die Lernenden weitere Beispiele in die Tabelle eintragen.

168

Present perfect: for, since

I Demonstration

Führen Sie das Thema ein, indem Sie über alte Fotos sprechen, z.B.

L: Do any of you like looking at old photos? (Geben Sie den Lernenden die Möglichkeit, kurz darauf einzugehen.)

Legen Sie die Folie auf den Tageslichtprojektor.

L: Look, this is Tony with his grandmother. They are looking at some old photos.

(Zeigen Sie auf Foto 1 und verändern Sie Ihre Stimme, um deutlich zu machen, daß zwei verschiedene Personen sprechen, Tony und seine Großmutter.)

Grandma says, »I haven't looked at these photos for years. That was at a party. I haven't been to a party since then, do you know? And I haven't danced for about fifteen years. Let's have a look at the others. (Zeigen Sie auf Foto 2): Oh look. That's the hat I bought for your Mum and Dad's wedding. I haven't worn it since 1957. I haven't bought a hat for years.

What's the next one? (Foto 3): Oh, good heavens! That's me on my bike. I haven't ridden a bike since I fell off it about twenty years ago.

What's this one? (Foto 4): Oh look, that was my first car. I bought it in 1951. I haven't driven a car for about three years.

Let's look at the next one. (Foto 5): Ah, that's my house. I've lived here for nearly fifty years. And that's my cat, Sammy. I've had him since last Christmas.

And what's this one? (Foto 6): Oh, that's when I went to Paris. I've not been there since 1949. And I haven't spoken French for years. That's an old friend. His name's Michael. I've known him all my life. I haven't seen him for a few years, though.«

II Verstehen und Reagieren

Gedächtnisspiel: Falschaussagen
Geben Sie den Lernenden die Gelegenheit, sich die Fotos einzuprägen. Machen Sie dann einige korrekte und bewußt falsche Aussagen über die Fotos. Die Schülerantworten beschränken sich auf *That's right/wrong.* Korrigieren Sie selbst Ihre »Falschaussagen«.

L: Look at these photos for a minute and try to remember them.
(Decken Sie die Bilder nach einer kurzen Zeit zu.)
Listen. Is this right or wrong? Tony's grandmother often looks at her photos.

S1: That's wrong.

L: Yes. She hasn't looked at them for years, has she?
Listen again: Grandma says she hasn't danced for about fifteen years.

S2: That's right.

L: Yes. Listen again: ...
usw.

Weitere »Falschaussagen«:
She's been to a lot of parties since 1950.
She's worn the hat about ten times since 1957.
She hasn't ridden a bike for two years.
She hasn't driven a car for about a year.
She says, »I've lived here since 1980.«
She's had her cat for two years.
She hasn't been to Paris since 1979.
She hasn't spoken French for about a year.
She's known Michael for five years.
But she hasn't seen him since Christmas.

III Reproduzieren

Kettenbilden
Legen Sie folgende Folie auf den Tageslichtprojektor oder benutzen Sie die Tafel. Lesen Sie die ersten beiden Sätze vor und lassen Sie den dritten Satz von den Lernenden vervollständigen.

L: Look at these sentences. »Mrs Blake first met Mr Collins in 1980. She has known him since 1980.« What else could you say?

S: She has known him for… years. (Die entsprechende Zahl wird von den Schülern eingesetzt.)

L: Look at number two: »The last time…«
usw.

---

1. Mrs Blake first met Mr Collins in 1980.
   She has known him since 1980.
   She .... for … years.

2. The last time Ben saw Penny was on Saturday. Today is Friday.
   He has not seen her since Saturday.
   .... for … days.

3. Carla went to live in America in 1954.
   She has been there for years.
   .... since …

4. The last time Carla spoke German was in 1954.
   She has not spoken German since 1954.
   .... for … years.

5. The last time Diane rode a horse was about ten years ago.
   She has not ridden a horse for ten years.
   .... since …

6. Jill bought a motor bike last April. It is October now.
   She has had it for six months.
   .... since …

7. Old Mr Hunter sold his car three months ago.
   He has not driven for three months.
   .... since …

8. Eric stopped buying sweets last Easter.
   He has not bought any sweets since then.
   .... for … months.

Lösungen:

1. She has known him for … years.
2. He has not seen her for six days.

3. She has been there since 1954.
4. She has not spoken German for ... years.
5. She has not ridden a horse since 19...
6. She has had it since April.
7. He has not driven since ...
8. He has not bought any sweets for ... months.

IV Produzieren

Bilder beschreiben
Ohne Hilfe des Lehrers beschreiben die Schüler die Fotos auf der ersten Folie.
  L: Look at these photos again. Let's see if you can talk about them now.
     What does Grandma say about the first one?
     »I haven't...?«
     usw.
Schreiben Sie folgende Strukturen als Hilfestellung an.

I	have ...	since 1950/...
	haven't ...	for ... years/months ...

V Bewußtmachung

For actions, states or situations that started sometime in the past and <u>still continue</u> we use the present perfect.

Jill has had her bike for six months. (= She still has it.)
Ben **has not seen** Penny since Saturday. (= He still has not seen her.)

<u>Note:</u> Germans often use the wrong tense. Be careful:
     Ich *kenne* ihn seit Jahren = I **have known** him for years.

For years/six months, three days, a while... – a **period** of time

Since 1957/I fell off my bike/Christmas... – a **specific** time in the past

Present perfect continuous

Legen Sie folgende Folie auf den Tageslichtprojektor.

Sally	Jenny	Dave	Ken	Sue
1.00	2.00	2.30	12.00	3.00

Steve	Helen	Tony	Anna	Neil
1.00	4.00	2.30	3.00	1.30

Norman	Mary	Peter	Cathy	Eric
4.30	1.30	3.30	4.00	12.00

I Demonstration

Die Bilder werden der Reihe nach unter Verwendung von *since* und *for* beschrieben.

L: I'm tired today. I've been teaching since (8.45).
Do you know, I've been teaching for (… hours).
Look at all these people. They're tired, too. It's five o'clock
in the afternoon and Sally's been driving since one.
She's been driving for four hours.
Jenny's been driving since two.
She's been driving for three hours.
usw.

Bildbeschreibung:
1. Reihe: *been driving*
2. Reihe: *been doing homework/working*
3. Reihe: *been working* gilt für alle; man kann aber auch differenzieren: *working in the garden/gardening, cooking, painting, working, working on a car*

II Verstehen und Reagieren

Geheime Auswahl
Suchen Sie eines der Bilder heraus, ohne zu verraten, an welche Person Sie denken. Nach Ihren Beschreibungen versuchen die Lernenden, die Person herauszufinden.

L: Listen carefully: This person has been doing homework since three o'clock. Who is it?
S: Anna.
L: That's right. Listen again: This person has been working for half an hour.
S: Norman.
usw.

Die Aufgabe wird schwieriger, wenn Sie für die 2. und 3. Reihe nur das Verb *work* gebrauchen.

III Reproduzieren

Falschaussagen
Machen Sie absichtlich falsche Aussagen über die Bilder. Dabei können Sie zwischen drei Arten von Falschaussagen wählen:
a) der Tätigkeit, z.B.
Sally has been doing homework since one o'clock.

174

b) der <u>Anfangszeit</u> der Tätigkeit, z.B.
   Sally has been driving since <u>two</u>.
c) der <u>Dauer</u> der Tätigkeit, z.B.
   Sally has been driving for <u>three and a half hours</u>.

L: Listen: Is this right or wrong? Peter has been painting since three o'clock.
S: It's wrong. He's been painting since half past three.
L: Yes, you're right. Listen again: …
   usw.
Diese Aktivität kann auch als Mannschaftswettbewerb organisiert werden.

IV Produzieren

Bilder beschreiben
Die Lernenden beschreiben die Bilder ohne Ihre Hilfe.
L: Let's see how much you've learned today. What can you say about all these people?
Schreiben Sie als Hilfestellung folgende Struktur auf:

| … has been …ing | since … |
| | for … hours. |

L: What can you say about Anna?
S: She's been doing homework/working since three.
L: And Mary?
S: She's been cooking for three and a half hours.
   usw.
Auch diese Aktivität kann als Wettbewerb organisiert werden.

V Bewußtmachung

Something has started and <u>is still going on now:</u>

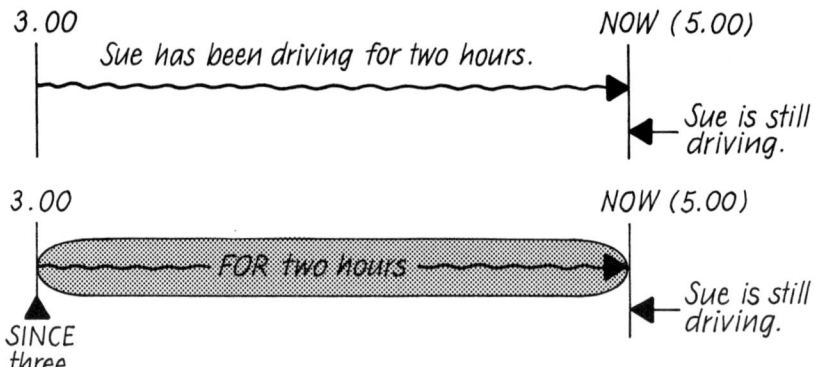

since – the time when something started: three o'clock, last Monday, 1986, April…

for – the period of time the action has been going on for: two hours, three days, five years, six months …

Relative clauses, shortened: there's a boy making a fire

I Demonstration

Führen Sie die Struktur *There's/are... ...ing* dadurch ein, daß Sie das Bild auf der Folie beschreiben.

    L: Look at this picture. There are lots of people doing all sorts of things, aren't there?
        There's a boy making a fire.
        There are two girls playing badminton.
        There's a girl climbing a tree.
        There's a dog chasing a cat.
        There's a woman lying on the grass.
        There's a man sitting on a chair.
        There's a boy picking flowers.
        There's a girl reading a magazine.

II Verstehen und Reagieren

Zuordnen
Auf der Grundlage Ihrer Beschreibungen benennen die Lernenden die verschiedenen Personen.

    L: Let's see who can answer these questions first.
        Who's the boy making a fire?
  S1: Martin.
    L: And who are the girls playing badminton?
  S2: Sheila and Kay.
      usw.

III Reproduzieren

Gedächtnisspiel
Die Schüler versuchen, das Bild aus dem Gedächtnis zu beschreiben. Die Aktivität kann auch als Mannschaftswettbewerb organisiert werden.
    L: Now look at the picture for a few minutes and try to remember it. But don't write anything down.
      (Nach einigen Minuten wird das Bild zugedeckt.)
      I'll tell you what I remember: There's a dog chasing a cat. What else?
Folgende Strukturen werden als Hilfestellung angeschrieben.

There is a	woman	
There are	two ...	...ing ...
	...	

  S1: There's a woman lying on the grass.
  S2: There are two girls playing badminton.
      usw.
Um die Struktur *Who's the ... ...ing ...?* zu üben, wird das Gedächtnisspiel wiederholt.
    L: Now we're going to play this game again. But this time I'm going to ask you different questions. Look at the picture for a few minutes and try to remember it.
      (Nach einigen Minuten wird das Bild zugedeckt.)
      Who's the man sitting on a chair?
  S1: Mr Bailey.
    L: That's right. Who can come here and ask the next question?
Schreiben Sie folgende Struktur an.

| Who is the | girl
... | ...ing ...? |

(S1) geht zum Tageslichtprojektor und schaut sich das Bild an.

L: You can ask, »Who's the woman lying on the grass?« or »Who are the boys looking out of the window?« or »Who's the girl climbing the tree?« and so on.

S1: Who's the girl reading a magazine?

S2: Sylvia.

S1: Yes.

L: Good. (That's one point for your team.) Who wants to come and ask the next question?

usw.

IV Produzieren

Anweisungen geben

Nach Anweisung der Lernenden entsteht ein zweites Bild an der Tafel bzw. auf einer neuen, leeren Folie. Die Szene kann wie im Demonstrationsbild in einem Garten oder aber in einem geschlossenen Raum, am Strand, im Zirkus, auf einem anderen belebten Platz etc. spielen. Wenn die Schüler selber Vorschläge für den Ort machen, haben sie eher das Gefühl, daran beteiligt zu sein.

L: Now we're going to draw a picture of our own. Shall we draw a picture of a garden or a beach or...?

Wenn man sich auf den Ort des Geschehens geeinigt hat, deuten Sie mit einfachen Strichzeichnungen einen Hintergrund an (Haus, Fenster, Tür, Tisch, Bäume, Meer, Zirkusarena usw.).

L: This looks a bit boring, doesn't it? We need some people doing things. Tell me what to draw. Say, »There's a ...« or »There are ...« (Deuten Sie auf die angeschriebenen Strukturen.)

S1: There's a girl swimming/reading a comic/eating...).

Auf jeden Vorschlag hin machen Sie eine entsprechende Strichzeichnung.

S2: There are two boys playing football.

usw.

Sie können weitere Anregungen geben, indem Sie einige Wörter anschreiben. Ermutigen Sie die Lernenden dazu, nach unbekanntem Wortschatz zu suchen bzw. zu fragen. Auch lustige Vorschläge können gemacht werden, z.B. *There's a monkey playing the piano.*

Um die Struktur *Who's the ... ...ing ...?* zu üben, bekommt jede auf dem fertigen Bild abgebildete Person einen Namen.

L: I think we've finished our picture now. Next we have to give all these people names.

(S1), come out here, please.

(Richten Sie die nächste Frage an S1): S1, who's the girl (wearing the bikini)?

S1: (Denkt sich einen englischen Namen aus) That's Jenny.

L: Write her name down then. Who wants to come out and write the next name down?

(Richten Sie die folgende Aufforderung an die Klasse): Ask (S2), »Who's the...?« (Deuten Sie auf die angeschriebene Struktur.)

S3: Who's the boy riding a horse?

S2: Johnny.

usw.

Auch hier können lustige Vorschläge gemacht werden, z.B. die Namen von Popsängern, Schauspielern usw.

V Bewußtmachung

After **there is/are/was/were** we often use the **-ing** form for **descriptions.**

> **There is** a girl climbing a tree.
> **There were** some people swimming in the sea.

To <u>find out who someone is</u> we often use the <u>-ing</u> form.

> **Who** is the man sitting on the chair?
> **Who** are those two boys playing badminton?

Die Schüler können weitere Beispiele aus der vorangegangenen Lektion geben.

Simple past: affirmative

Legen Sie folgende Folie auf den Tageslichtprojektor oder zeichnen Sie das Diagramm an die Tafel. Der Wortschatz kann der jeweiligen Klasse angepaßt werden.

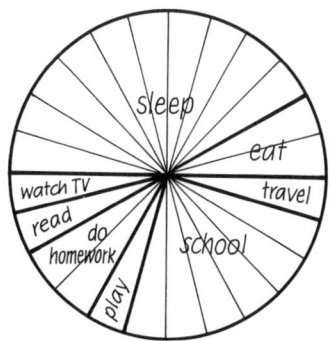

I Demonstration

Führen Sie einige der im Diagramm genannten Verben in der *simple past*-Form kurz ein, indem Sie erzählen, was Sie gestern nach der Schule gemacht haben.

L: When I got home from school yesterday I was very tired. First I *slept* for an hour. Then I *ate* a sandwich. After that I *read* the paper. Then I *played* (the violin/some records/with my son…). After that I *did* some marking. Then I *watched* TV.

Während der Besprechung des Diagramms schreiben Sie die *simple past*-Formen an.

L: Look at this diagram. This is what Philip did yesterday. He slept for ten hours. He travelled to school and back again for an hour. He was in school for six hours. He ate for two hours: he ate breakfast for half an hour; he ate lunch for half an hour and he ate his tea for an hour. He played with his friends for an hour. He did homework for two hours. He read for an hour and he watched TV for an hour.

II Verstehen und Reagieren

Diagramm erstellen
Ein ähnliches Diagramm wird für eine zweite Person erstellt. Teilen Sie dazu folgendes zweites Diagramm aus. Nach Ihren Beschreibungen malen die Schüler die dick umrandeten Felder verschiedenfarbig aus.

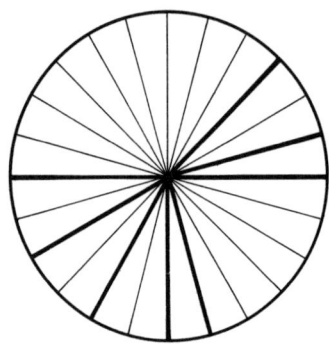

L: Now this is a diagram for a girl called Mary. Yesterday she slept for nine hours. Let's colour those nine hours yellow. She ate for two hours – let's colour them red. She travelled for an hour – let's take green for that. She was in school for five hours – let's say orange. She played the flute for an hour – colour that brown. She did homework for two hours – let's take pink for that. She played with friends for two hours – colour those two hours blue. And she watched TV for two hours – let's use black.

III Reproduzieren

Information erfragen und erteilen
Vergleichen Sie die Zeit, die Sie und die Lernenden am Vortag für die angegebenen Tätigkeiten gebraucht haben. Sprechen Sie die jeweilige *simple past*-Form vor.
  L: I slept for … hours yesterday. What about you?
  S1: I slept for … (Geben Sie mehreren Schülern die Gelegenheit, darauf zu antworten.)
  L: I ate/travelled to school and back/was in school/played (the piano/records/ with …)/did some marking (S: did homework)/read/watched TV for … hours. What about you?
     usw.

IV Produzieren

Diagramme erstellen und darüber berichten
Die Schüler erstellen für sich selbst ein ähnliches Diagramm. Teilen Sie dazu leere Diagramme ohne dick umrandete Felder aus.

L: Think about what you did yesterday and colour your diagram, like we did for Mary. When you've finished, write down what you did.

Schreiben Sie als Hilfestellung folgende *simple past*-Formen an:

I slept/ate/travelled/was in school/played.../did homework/read/ watched TV.

Wenn die Diagramme fertig sind, berichten die Schüler über ihren gestrigen Tag: *Yesterday I slept for... hours. I ate for...* usw.

V Bewußtmachung

Nachdem Sie die Regel erklärt haben, lassen Sie die Lernenden Beispiele für *simple past*-Formen aus der vorausgegangenen Lektion finden.

If we want to talk about something which happened at a <u>specific time in the past</u> – yesterday, at three o'clock, last year, two months ago... – we use the <u>simple past</u> tense.

There are special simple past forms of the different verbs:

infinitive	simple past form
to sleep	....
to travel	....
to be (in school)	....
to eat	....
to play	....
to do (homework)	....
to read	....
to watch (TV)	....

It's easy to remember the simple past forms of some verbs because you only have to add »-ed« to the infinitive. Can you find some examples from this list? (travel – Weisen Sie auf die Verdoppelung des Endkonsonanten hin, play, watch)

Sie können weitere Beispiele für regelmäßige und unregelmäßige Verben hinzufügen, auch *simple past*-Formen, bei denen der Endkonsonant verdoppelt wird. Weitere Beispiele:

Regelmäßige Verben – answer, arrive, ask, clean, talk, use, visit, wash, work.

Unregelmäßige Verben – obige Liste: ate, did, read, slept, was.

Weitere: buy, come, get, give, go, have, say, see, tell, write.

Verdoppelung des Endkonsonanten: plan, stop.

Simple past: negative

I Demonstration

Führen Sie einige der Verben, die auf der Folie oder an der Tafel erscheinen, in der Präsensform kurz ein oder wiederholen Sie sie.

L: We do the same things every day, don't we? We *get up* at the same time, we *have* the same things for breakfast. We often *wear* the same kind of clothes – say, always jeans or something. We *go* to school, then we do the same kind of things in the evenings and so on.

Sprechen Sie über die folgende Tabelle.

LAST WEEK	YESTERDAY
Got up at 7.30	didn't get up 7.30 – 8.00
Had toast for breakfast	didn't have – muesli
Wore trousers	didn't wear – skirt
Went to school by bus	didn't go – by bike
Talked during lessons	didn't talk
Played basketball after school	didn't play – badminton
Read comics in the evenings	didn't read – a novel

L: This is Carol. She does the same things every day, too. All last week she got up at half past seven, had toast for breakfast, wore trousers, went to school by bus. She talked during lessons. After school she always played basketball and every evening she read comics.

But yesterday was different. You see, yesterday was her birthday and she wanted her birthday to be different. So she didn't get up at half past seven, but at eight. She didn't have toast for breakfast, but muesli.
usw.

184

II Verstehen und Reagieren

Information erteilen
Benennen Sie die Tätigkeiten, die Carol anläßlich ihres gestrigen Geburtstages ausnahmsweise nicht ausführte. Die Schüler ergänzen, was Carol anstatt dessen tatsächlich tat. Vermeiden Sie die Frage *»What did she do?«* zu diesem frühen Zeitpunkt, da sie die Lernenden zu falschen Strukturen wie z.B.* *»She didn't do get up«* verleiten kann.

    L: Yesterday Carol didn't go to school by bus, she…?
   S1:   Went by bike.
    L: And she didn't play basketball after school, she…?
   S2:   Played badminton.
        usw.

III Reproduzieren

Geheime Auswahl
Teilen Sie folgendes Arbeitsblatt aus.

Abwechselnd suchen sich die Lernenden eine der abgebildeten Personen aus. Die Wahl wird dem Lehrer, nicht aber der Klasse mitgeteilt. Anhand bestimmter Hinweise, die Sie dem jeweiligen Schüler zuflüstern, spricht dieser zu seinen Mitschülern, die die gesuchte Person herauszufinden versuchen.
Erklären Sie zunächst alle Symbole.

L: Yesterday it was all these people's birthdays. Like Carol, they all wanted their birthdays to be different.
Lynne, for instance, didn't get up early. She didn't make breakfast and she didn't do the washing up.
What about Jane? She didn't get up early, either. She didn't do the washing up and she didn't clean the house.
And Rosie? She didn't...
usw.

L: Now (S1), come out here and think of one of these people. But don't say who. Write her name down, so I know. The others can ask three questions to find out who you're thinking of.
(Flüstern Sie S1, der z.B. an Diane denkt, die Negativsätze zu): Say, »She didn't get up early, she didn't do the washing up and she didn't work in the garden«.
S1: She didn't get up ... in the garden.
S2: Rosie?
L: No. Listen again. (S1 wiederholt seine Hinweise.)
S3: Diane?
S1: That's right.
L: Now you come out here (S3).
usw.

Das Fragespiel kann auch als Mannschaftswettbewerb organisiert werden.

IV Produzieren

Geheime Auswahl
Das Spiel wird in Partnerarbeit fortgesetzt.

L: Now you need a partner. First partner A thinks of one of these people. Partner B can only ask three questions. If partner B is right, then he or she thinks of the next person. But if partner B can't guess who it is in three questions then partner A can think of a second person.

V Bewußtmachung

Nachdem Sie die Regel gegeben haben, lassen Sie die Lernenden weitere Beispiele aus der vorausgegangenen Lektion finden.

All week Carol *got up* early. Yesterday she **did not get** up early.

did not + infinitive

All week Lynne .... Yesterday she ....

Simple past: questions with question words:
what/when did you...?

Legen Sie folgende Folie auf den Tageslichtprojektor oder benutzen Sie die Tafel.

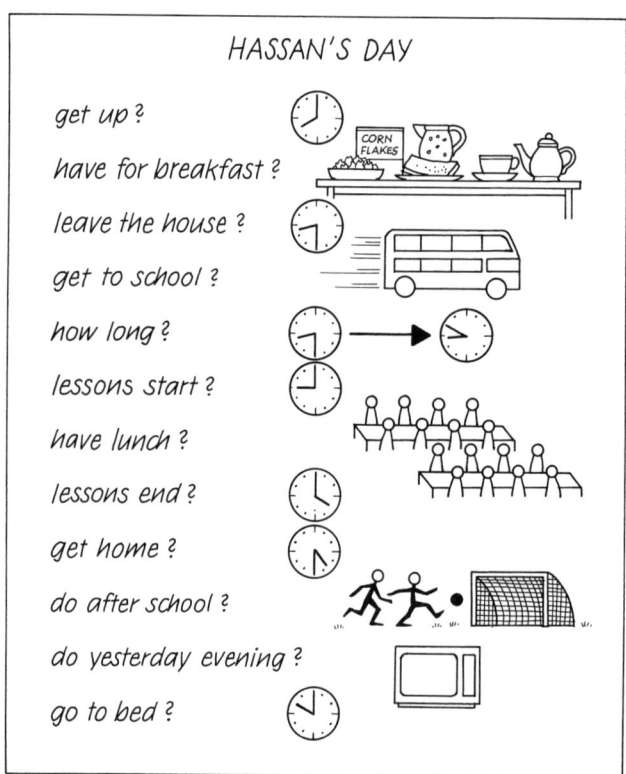

I Demonstration

Führen Sie das Thema ein, indem Sie über den heutigen Tagesanfang sprechen.
Verwenden Sie aber die neue Struktur noch nicht.

L: I got up at... this morning. What about you? (Geben Sie den Lernenden die
     Gelegenheit, kurz darauf zu antworten.)

S1: I got up at...

S2: ...

L: I left the house at... And you?

S3: I left at...

S4: ...

Besprechen Sie nun die Folie.

L: Hassan is an English boy and he goes to school in Leeds, in the North of England. Let's see what he did yesterday.
What time did he get up? – Eight o'clock. You know that school starts later in England, don't you?
What did he have for breakfast? – Cornflakes, toast and a cup of tea.
When did he leave the house? – Half past eight.
How did he get to school? – By bus.
How long did it take? – Twenty minutes.
What time did lessons start? – Nine o'clock.
Where did Hassan have lunch yesterday? – At school.
What time did lessons end? – At four.
When did Hassan get home? – At half past four.
What did he do after school? – He played football.
What did he do yesterday evening? – He watched TV.
And when did he go to bed? – At ten.

II Verstehen und Reagieren

Fragebogen ausfüllen
Teilen Sie folgenden Fragebogen aus. Legen Sie einen Bogen als Folie auf den Tageslichtprojektor und füllen Sie die Spalte »me« während dieser Phase aus.

Questionnaire		
What did you do yesterday?		
	me	**my partner**
	Name: _____	Name: _____
1. What time did you get up yesterday?	_____	_____
2. What did you have for breakfast?	_____	_____
3. When did you leave the house?	_____	_____
4. How did you get to school?	_____	_____
5. How long did it take?	_____	_____
6. What time did you get home?	_____	_____
7. What did you do after school?	_____	_____
8. What did you do yesterday evening?	_____	_____
9. When did you go to bed?	_____	_____
10. How long did you sleep?	_____	_____

Lesen Sie die Fragen vor. Die Schüler beantworten sie mündlich und schriftlich.

L: This is a questionnaire. Let's find out about everybody here, shall we?
Look at the first question: »What time did you get up yesterday?«
(Geben Sie einigen Schülern die Gelegenheit, darauf zu antworten.)

S1: At...

S2: ...

usw.

L: Let's fill in the answer, then. Write it under »me«. (Füllen Sie die Antwort auf der Folie für Ihre Person aus.)
Now what's the next question? »What did you have for breakfast?«
usw.

III Reproduzieren

Information erfragen und erteilen

Jede auf dem Fragebogen erscheinende Frage wird zuerst vom Lehrer an einen Schüler gerichtet, danach fragen sich die Schüler gegenseitig.

L: (S1), what time did you get up yesterday?

S1: ...

L: Ask someone else.

S1: (S2), what time did you get up yesterday?
usw.

IV Produzieren

Information erfragen und erteilen

In Partnerarbeit wird die Spalte »**my partner**« ausgefüllt.

L: Now you need a partner. First one partner asks all these questions and writes the answers down under »my partner«. Then the other partner asks the questions and writes the answers down.

Die Schülerpaare tauschen die ausgefüllten Fragebogen untereinander aus, so daß jedes Schülerpaar die Bogen eines anderen Paares vorliegen hat. Über die Ergebnisse wird dann berichtet.

L: (S1), whose names are on your questionnaire?

S1: (S7) and (S13).

L: What time did (S7) get up yesterday?

S1: (Liest die Eintragung vor.)

L (Wenden Sie sich an die Klasse): Now you ask, »What time did (S13) get up yesterday?«

S2: What time did (S13) get up yesterday?

S1: ...

L: (Sprechen Sie zur Klasse. Als Sprechimpuls deuten Sie auf die Fragen der Folie.) Go on.

S3: What did (S7) have for breakfast?

S1: ...

S4: What did (S13) have for breakfast?

S1: ...

S5: When did (S7) leave the house?

usw.

V Bewußtmachung

When we ask questions about something that happened at a specific time in the past and we use a question word, we need the verb »to do«.

question word + did + infinitive

What (time)		he	get up?
When	did	you	have for breakfast?
How (long)		they	go to bed?
Where		...	...?

Lassen Sie die Schüler weitere Beispiele aus der vorausgegangenen Lektion finden.

Simple past: questions without question words: did you...?

I Demonstration

Führen Sie die neuen Strukturen und ggf. die unbekannten Wörter ein, indem Sie einige kleine Merkzettel aus Ihren Taschen holen. Der Wortschatz soll der jeweiligen Lerngruppe angepaßt sein.

L: Look at all these bits of paper. What's this one? (Lesen Sie einen der Zettel vor.) »Collect coat from cleaner's.« Did I collect it? No, I didn't. I forgot. (Holen Sie weitere Zettel aus Ihren Taschen und kommentieren Sie sie in ähnlicher Weise.) What's this one? »Visit Eric in hospital.« Did I visit him? Yes, I did – last Wednesday.
usw.

L: I always write down everything I have to do, do you?
(Geben Sie den Lernenden die Möglichkeit, kurz darauf zu antworten, bevor Sie die folgende Folie auf den Tageslichtprojektor auflegen oder auf folgendes Tafelbild zeigen.)

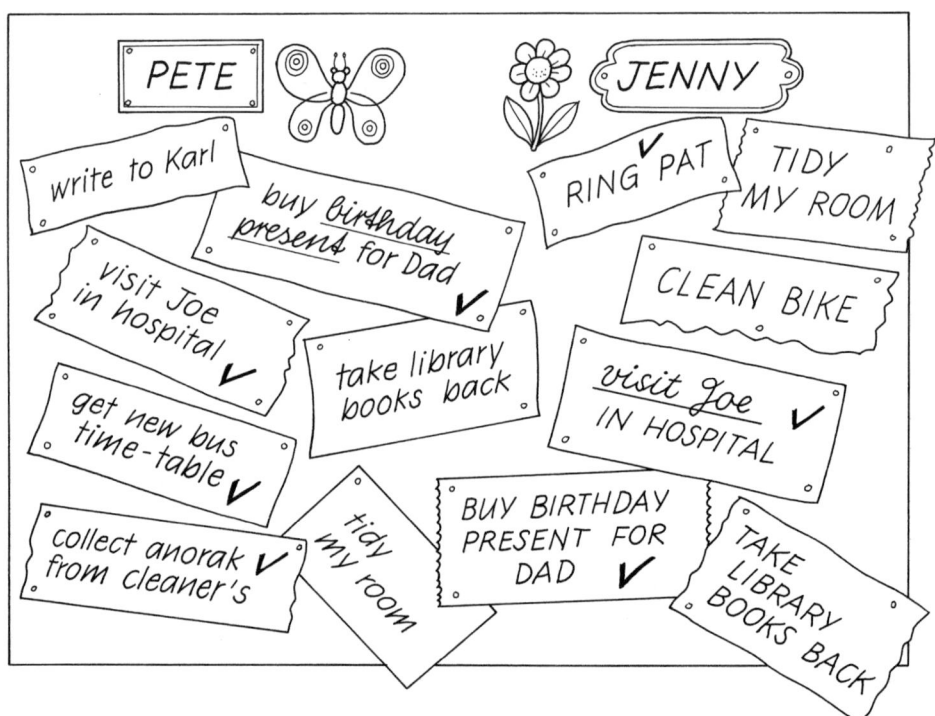

L: Pete and Jenny write everything down, too. They put notes on this board. Last week there were a lot of notes – a lot of things they wanted to do. Let's see if they did everything. Did Pete write to Karl? – No, he didn't. Did he buy a birthday present for his father? – Yes, he did. usw.

Auf diese Weise werden alle Merkzettel besprochen.

II Verstehen und Reagieren

Information erfragen und erteilen
Legen Sie folgende zweite Folie auf den Tageslichtprojektor.

Mother:	Did you collect your anorak from the cleaner's last week?
.........:	Yes, I did.
Mother:	Did you clean your bike last week?
.........:	No, I didn't.
Mother:	Did you get a new bus time-table?
.........:	Yes, I did.
Mother:	Did you take your library books back?
.........:	No, we didn't.
Mother:	Did you buy a present for your father?
.........:	Yes, we did.
Mother:	Did you write to Karl?
.........:	No, I didn't.
Mother:	Did you ring Pat?
.........:	Yes, I did.
Mother:	Did you visit Joe in hospital?
.........:	Yes, we did.
Mother:	Did you tidy your rooms?
.........:	No, we didn't.

L: Pete and Jenny's mother knows that her children often forget to do things. So she always asks them about their notes. (Lesen Sie die erste Frage): »Did you collect your anorak from the cleaner's last week?« Look at the answer. Do you know who said that? Pete, Jenny or both?

S1: Pete.

L: Yes, he did. Pete said it. So let's write his name down. (Tragen Sie die Namen im Laufe des Gesprächs ein.)
    Then she asks, »Did you clean your bike last week?« The answer is, »No, I didn't.« Who said that?

S2: Jenny.

L: Yes, she did. That's right.
     usw.

Lösungen:
Pete/Jenny/Pete/Both/Both/Pete/Jenny/Both/Both

III Reproduzieren

Information erfragen und erteilen
Die Strukturen werden in einem Rollenspiel geübt. Nachdem Sie das Gespräch
mit einem Schüler vorgeführt haben, übernehmen die Lernenden beide Rollen.
Flüstern Sie den Sprechern die Strukturen ins Ohr. Jede »Mutter« bzw. jeder
»Vater« stellt zwei Fragen.

L: Let's imagine I'm Pete and Jenny's mother/father. Who wants to be Pete?
     Now (S1), you're Pete. Well, my son, I know you often forget things, don't
     you? What about last week? Did you take your library books back? (Flü-
     stern Sie ihm die Antwort ins Ohr.)
S1: No, I didn't.
L: And did you collect your anorak?
S1: Yes, I did.
L: Good. So you remembered that. Now let's have two more people, one for
     the mother or father and one for Jenny. Now (S2, als Elternteil), ask Jenny,
     »Did you ring…?« or »Did you…?« (Als Sprechimpuls deuten Sie auf die
     Liste.)
S2: Did you visit Joe in hospital?
S3: (als Jenny) Yes, I did.
S2: And did you…?
     usw.

IV Produzieren

Information erfragen und erteilen
Teilen Sie folgende zwei Arbeitsblätter an Schülerpaare aus. Nachdem die Schüler
einige Zeit geübt haben, können sie ihre Gespräche der Klasse vorführen.

Partner A	Partner B
Last Easter Maria and Kate went to London together. They visited the Tower of London and a lot of other places. Kate took photos. She didn't write postcards and she didn't buy presents or souvenirs.	Last Easter Maria and Kate went to London together. They visited Buckingham Palace. Maria didn't take photos. She wrote two postcards and she bought a present for her brother – a book. She didn't buy souvenirs.
Ask your partner:	Your partner is going to ask you a question.
1. Did they visit Buckingham Palace?	1. Answer *Yes, they did* or *No, they didn't.*
2. Now answer your partner's questions with *Yes, they did* or *No, they didn't.*	2. Now you ask, »Did they visit the Tower of London?«
3. Photos? Did Maria take…?	3. Yes, she did/No, she didn't.
4. Yes, she did/No, she didn't.	4. Kate? …Kate… photos?
5. Postcards? …Maria write postcards?	5. Yes, …/No, …
6. Yes, …/No, …	6. Kate? …Kate …postcards?
7. Presents? …Maria buy p…?	7. Yes,…(Say what it was)/ No, …
8. Yes, …/No, …	8. Kate? …Kate …p…?
9. Souvenirs? …Maria …s…?	9. …
10. …	10. Kate? …Kate …s…?
Now give your partner this piece of paper and start again.	Now give your partner this piece of paper and start again.

V Bewußtmachung

Erklären Sie die Regel und lassen Sie dann die Lernenden weitere Beispiele aus der vorausgegangenen Lektion finden.

To ask questions about something that happened at a <u>specific</u> time in the past we need

did	+	infinitive

	Maria	take	photos?
Did	Pete	write	to Karl?
	the children	visit	Joe?
	…	…	…?

Find some more examples.

To answer questions like this we say

	Yes, I/she/they… **did**
or	
	No, I/she/they… **didn't**

196

Simple present: affirmative: I/you work

Die 1. Person Sing. wird aktiv, die 2. Person Sing. passiv gelernt.

I Demonstration

Um zu verdeutlichen, daß zwei Personen sprechen, benutzt der Lehrer Handpuppen oder zeichnet zwei Figuren an die Tafel und variiert seine Stimme.

L: Look (deuten Sie auf die Handpuppen oder die zwei Figuren an der Tafel), this is Brian and this is Sally. They are talking. Listen.

B: Hello, Sally. How are you?

S: Fine, thanks. And you?

B: Fine. I've got a new job.

S: Have you? What is it?

B: Can you guess? I wear uniform, I travel a lot and I talk to a lot of people.

S: Let me think. You wear uniform, you travel a lot and you talk to a lot of people. A tourist guide?

B: No, try again.

S: Give me some help, then.

B: All right. I drive.

S: You drive. Let me think: You wear uniform, you travel a lot, you talk to a lot of people and you drive. I know. A taxi driver.

B: No, but nearly.

S: A bus driver?

B: That's right.

II Verstehen und Reagieren

Geheime Auswahl
Legen Sie folgende Folie auf den Tageslichtprojektor.

L: Look at all these people. They all have different jobs. There's a secretary, a cook, a waiter, a doctor, an air hostess, a policeman, a journalist, a housewife, a nurse and a mechanic. Now listen. Let's say I'm one of these people. Can you guess who I am?
In my job I write a lot. I work indoors and outdoors, too.
S: A policeman?
L: No, try again. Listen: I write a lot, I work indoors and outdoors.
S: A journalist?
L: Yes. Now listen again. I...
usw.

Während dieses Schrittes werden die folgenden Vokabeln eingeführt bzw. wiederholt. Schreiben Sie die in der linken Spalte aufgeführten Tätigkeitsmerkmale in der vorgegebenen Reihenfolge an die Tafel. Die in Klammern angegebenen Berufe geben Ihnen einen schnellen Überblick über die Zuordnung verschiedener Berufe zu den einzelnen Tätigkeitsmerkmalen. Ordnen Sie jeweils *einen* dieser Berufe den Merkmalen zu, z.B. *write a lot – journalist.*

write a lot	(secretary, journalist, policeman)
work indoors	(all)
work outdoors	(journalist, policeman)
work with food	(cook, waiter, air hostess, housewife, nurse)
talk to a lot of people	(secretary, waiter, doctor, journalist, air hostess, policeman)
do things for others	(secretary, cook, waiter, doctor, air hostess, policeman, housewife, mechanic, nurse)
travel a lot	(journalist, air hostess)
wear uniform	(cook, waiter, doctor, air hostess, policeman, nurse)
repair things	(housewife, mechanic)
make things	(cook, housewife, mechanic)
make tea	(secretary, air hostess, housewife, nurse)

III Reproduzieren

Da die Struktur den Lernenden keine große Schwierigkeit bereitet, kann dieser Schritt ausgelassen werden.

IV Produzieren

Geheime Auswahl

L: I want someone to come out here. (Ein Schüler kommt heraus.) Now let's say you are one of the people in the picture. Don't tell us who you are. But tell us about your job. Say, »I wear uniform« or »I work outdoors«. (Deuten Sie auf die Vokabeln an der Tafel.)

S1: I work with food.

S2: A cook?

S1: No.

S3: A waiter?

S1: No.

L: You can say, »Give us more help, please«.

S4: Give us more help, please.

S1: I travel a lot.

S5: An air hostess?

S1: Yes.

Dieser Dialog wird nun in Partnerarbeit geübt. Fortgeschrittene Klassen können nach Belieben weitere Berufe und Tätigkeitsmerkmale hinzufügen und sich darüber befragen.

V Bewußtmachung

For things we do <u>regularly,</u> for example in our <u>jobs,</u> we use the simple present.

I	**wear**	uniform.
You	**work**	indoors.

Simple present: affirmative: she/he plays

Legen Sie folgende Folie auf den Tageslichtprojektor.

I Demonstration

Die Bilder symbolisieren die Freizeitbeschäftigungen der einzelnen Personen: *playing volleyball, playing table tennis, going for bike rides, going for walks, reading books, reading comics.*

    L: Look at all these people. They all have hobbies, or things that they do in their spare time. Look at Dave. He plays volleyball, sometimes he goes for walks and sometimes he reads books.

           What about Ann? She plays table tennis, she goes for walks and...

           usw.

II Verstehen und Reagieren

Geheime Auswahl
Beschreiben Sie die Freizeitbeschäftigungen jeweils einer im Arbeitsblatt abgebildeten Person, ohne den Namen zu nennen. Die Schüler müssen den Namen der Person herausfinden.

L: Now listen. Who am I thinking of? This person goes for walks and reads books. Who is it?
S1: Tony?
L: No. Listen again: He goes for walks and he reads books.
S2: Dave?
L: That's right. This time I'm thinking of a girl. She goes for bike rides and she…
usw.

III Reproduzieren

Falschaussagen
Die Bilder werden zugedeckt. Um die Lernenden zu Aussagen über die Freizeitbeschäftigungen der einzelnen Personen zu bewegen, verwechselt der Lehrer absichtlich folgende Paare von Beschäftigungen:

playing table tennis	–	*playing volleyball*
going for bike rides	–	*going for walks*
reading books	–	*reading comics*

Um die Aufgabe etwas schwieriger zu machen, sollten einige Lehreräußerungen inhaltlich korrekt sein.

L: Now I'll give you a few minutes to look at these pictures. Try to remember them. Tell yourself, Dave: volleyball, walks, books, or Lynne: table tennis, goes for bike rides, comics and so on. Don't write anything down. Start now.
(Geben Sie den Lernenden eine Denkpause.)
Now (die Bilder werden abgedeckt), let's see how much you can remember. Listen: Dave plays volleyball. Is that right or wrong?
S1: That's right.
L: Yes. Look. (Das Bild von Dave wird kurz aufgedeckt.)
Now listen again: Sue plays table tennis. Is that right or wrong?
S2: That's right.
L: Are you sure? What do the others think?
S3: No, it's wrong.
L: She plays…?

S4: Volleyball.

L: Yes. She plays volleyball. Look. (Das Bild wird kurz aufgedeckt.) Now listen again: Pete reads comics...
usw.

IV Produzieren

Information erteilen

L: Now look at these pictures and tell me about all these people. Let's start with Dave. What can you tell me about him?

S1: He plays volleyball, he goes for walks and he reads books.

L: That's right. Now what about Ann?
usw.

Geheime Auswahl

Die Schüler spielen in Partnerarbeit das unter II vorgeführte Ratespiel, wobei abwechselnd ein Schüler die dort vom Lehrer vertretene Rolle übernimmt.

L: Now you need a partner. One of you thinks of somebody in the picture. But don't tell your partner the person's name. Say, »He goes for walks and he reads comics. Who is it?« or »She plays table tennis, she goes for bike rides and she reads comics. Who is it?«
When your partner knows who it is start again. This time your partner thinks of somebody in the picture.

S1: She plays volleyball and she reads books. Who is it?

S2: Sue?

S1: Yes.

S2: He goes for walks...
usw.

V Bewußtmachung

For things we do <u>regularly,</u> like hobbies, we use the <u>simple present.</u>

Dave **plays** volleyball.
Jean and Frank **go** for bike rides.

Simple present: negative: she/he doesn't; they don't

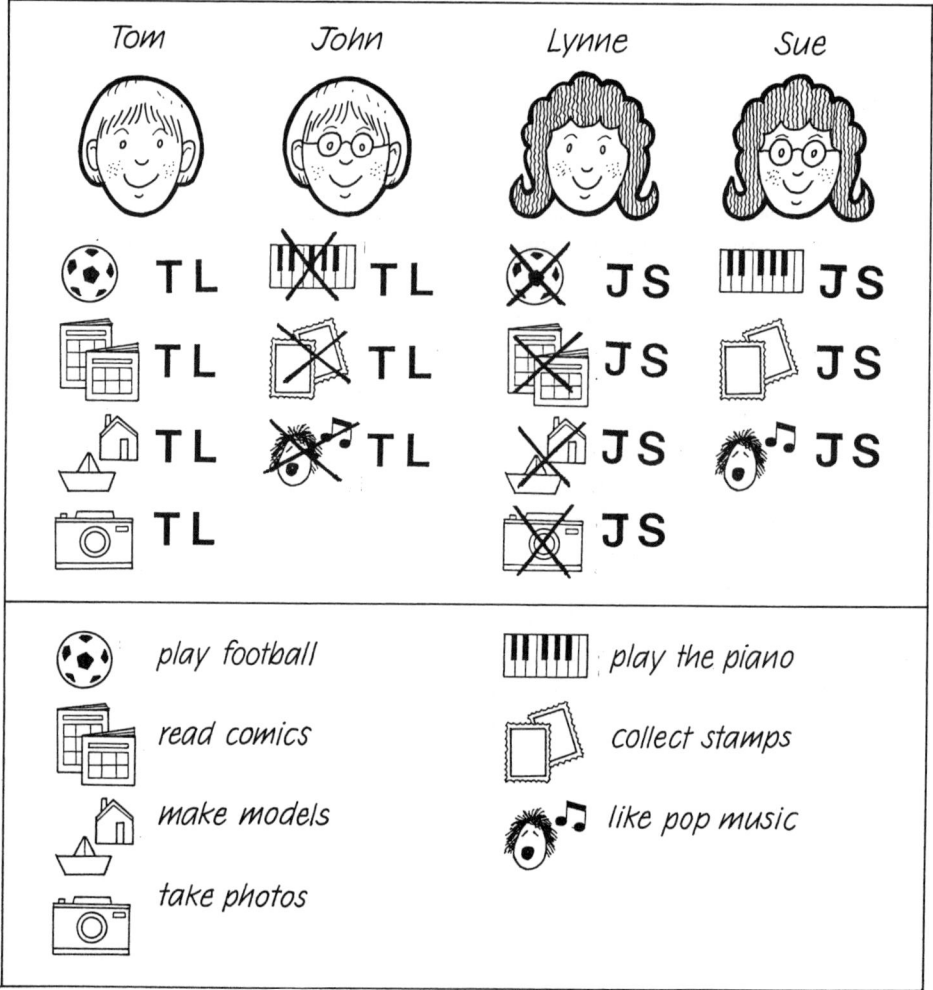

Die großen Anfangsbuchstaben stehen für die vier abgebildeten Personen. Durchgestrichene Symbole bedeuten, daß die betreffenden Personen diesen Hobbys nicht nachgehen.

Um die Bedeutung der Negativformen *doesn't* und *don't* klarzumachen, werden sie zusammen mit den entsprechenden Affirmativformen eingeführt. Sie sollten jedoch isoliert geübt werden, um die falsche Struktur* *he doesn't plays* zu vermeiden.

Doesn't

I Demonstration

Legen Sie die Folie auf den Tageslichtprojektor oder benutzen Sie die Tafel. Die Bilder der zwei Mädchen werden zugedeckt.

L: Look at these two boys. They're twins, aren't they? They look the same – well, nearly the same. Tom doesn't wear glasses. They have different interests and hobbies, too. (Deuten Sie auf die entsprechenden Symbole und Buchstaben): T means »Tom« and J means »John«. Tom plays football, he reads comics, he makes models and he takes photos.
John doesn't play football, he doesn't read comics, he doesn't make models and he doesn't take photos. He has different interests. He plays the piano, he collects stamps and he likes pop music.

II Verstehen und Reagieren

Geheime Auswahl
Decken Sie die Bilder der zwei Mädchen auf. Auf der Grundlage Ihrer Beschreibungen versuchen die Lernenden herauszufinden, an welche Person Sie denken. Beschreiben Sie zunächst eines der Mädchen, dann eine der vier Personen. Verwenden Sie dabei immer die Negativform *doesn't*.

L: Here are two more twins, Lynne and Sue. L means »Lynne« and S means »Sue«. Listen. I'll tell you about one of these girls. She doesn't read comics. Which girl is that?
S1: Sue.
L: That's right. Sue doesn't read comics. (Wiederholen Sie jedesmal die richtige Antwort.) Now who am I thinking of: He doesn't make models.
S2: John.
usw.

Das Ratespiel wird so lange wie nötig fortgesetzt.
Beschreibungen der Mädchen:
Lynne – doesn't wear glasses, play the piano, collect stamps, like pop music;
Sue – doesn't play football, read comics, make models, take photos.

III Reproduzieren

Information geben
Die Zwillingsbrüder werden miteinander verglichen.

L: John doesn't have the same hobbies as his brother. He doesn't play football and…? (Deuten Sie auf die durchgestrichenen Symbole als Sprechimpulse.)

S1: He doesn't read comics.

S2: He doesn't make models.

S3: He doesn't take photos.

L: And Tom doesn't have the same interests as John. He doesn't play the piano …?

S4: He doesn't collect stamps.

S5: He doesn't like pop music.

L: And look at the girls. Lynne doesn't have the same hobbies as her sister. (Deuten Sie auf die entsprechenden Symbole.) She doesn't play the piano …?

S6: She doesn't collect stamps.

S7: She doesn't like pop music.

L: And Sue doesn't have the same interests as Lynne either. She doesn't…? usw.

IV Produzieren

Gedächtnisspiel
Die Folie wird zugedeckt. Die Schüler sollen mit Hilfe der neuen Struktur die Hobbys und Interessen beschreiben, denen eine bestimmte Person *nicht* nachgeht. Vermeiden Sie zu diesem frühen Zeitpunkt den Fragetyp *Does he…?*, da er zu innersprachlichen Interferenzen führen kann.

L: Now I'm going to cover the pictures up. What can you remember about Tom? What about the piano?

S1: He doesn't play the piano.

L: Yes, you're right. Tom doesn't play the piano. And what about stamps?

S2: He doesn't collect stamps.
   usw.

Je nach Leistungsstand der Klasse kann auch die Affirmativform mit verwendet werden.

Don't

Die gleiche Folie kann auch für die Einführung bzw. Wiederholung von *don't* verwendet werden.

I Demonstration

L: Look at these four people. They're twins, aren't they? But they haven't got the same hobbies and interests. They're very different. (Deuten Sie auf die entsprechenden Symbole.) Look, Tom and Lynne play football, they read comics, they make models and they take photos.
But look at Tom's brother and Lynne's sister:
John and Sue don't play football, they don't read comics, they don't make models and they don't take photos.

Weitere Beispielsätze:
John and Sue play the piano, collect stamps, like pop music; Tom and Lynne don't play the piano, collect stamps, like pop music.

II Verstehen und Reagieren

Geheime Auswahl
Gehen Sie vor wie bei *doesn't*, aber beschreiben Sie jeweils zwei Personen mit den gleichen Interessen (Tom und Lynne oder John und Sue) anstatt nur eine.

L: Listen. I'm thinking of two of these people: They don't collect stamps.

III Reproduzieren

Information geben
Wie bei *doesn't*, jedoch mit dem Unterschied, daß zwei Personen mit den gleichen Interessen beschrieben werden.

L: John and Sue don't have the same interests as Tom and Lynne. They don't play football and…?

IV Produzieren

Gedächtnisspiel
Wie bei *doesn't*, aber diesmal werden zwei Personen mit den gleichen Interessen beschrieben.

L: What can you remember about John and Sue? What about comics?
S1: They don't read comics.
       usw.

V Bewußtmachung

For things that people do <u>regularly,</u> like <u>hobbies,</u> and for people's <u>interests</u> we use
the simple present.
To say that someone does not have a certain hobby we use

<u>**does/do not** + **infinitive**</u>

Tom	**does not**	**collect** stamps.
Tom and Lynne	**do not**	**like** pop music.

Simple present: interrogative: does she/he…?
short answers: yes, she/he does;
no, she/he doesn't

Teilen Sie folgendes Arbeitsblatt aus. Sie können die Tabelle auch als Folie auf den Tageslichtprojektor legen.

	play tennis	collect stamps	take photos	like pop music	classic-al music	paint	write letters
Cathy		✔		✔			✔
Ralph	✔		✔		✔	✔	
Angela							
Martin							
Diane							

In dieser Unterrichtseinheit wird folgender Wortschatz verwendet:
to play tennis, to collect stamps, to take photos, to like pop/classical music, to paint, to write letters; box of paints, book about painting/photography/a pop star, cassette, photo album, picture/poster of a pop star, record, socks, stamp album, tennis balls, writing paper.
Der Wortschatz kann dem Kenntnisstand der jeweiligen Klasse angepaßt werden, indem man einzelne Hobbys und die zugeordneten Geschenke entweder wegläßt oder durch andere ersetzt.

I Demonstration

Im Laufe der Lehrerdemonstration kann unbekannter Wortschatz wie folgt einge-führt werden. Die Haken zeigen an, an welchen Aktivitäten die jeweilige Person interessiert ist.

L: Look at these people. It's their birthdays soon and we want to get some presents for them. Let's see what they're interested in. What about Cathy? (Zeigen Sie auf die Tabelle):
Does she play tennis? – No, she doesn't. Does she collect stamps? Yes, she does. So what about (zeigen Sie auf die Geschenke) a stamp album? Or maybe something else?
(Zeigen Sie auf die Tabelle): Does she takes photos? – No, she doesn't. Does she like pop music? – Yes, she does. So why not get her a record or a cassette or a poster of a pop star?
Does she like classical music? – No, she doesn't.
usw.
(Es werden nur die Interessen von Cathy besprochen.)

II Verstehen und Reagieren

Zuordnen
Die Geschenke werden den Interessen der verschiedenen Personen zugeordnet.

L: Now let's try to find a present for Ralph. (Zeigen Sie auf die Tabelle): Does he play tennis? – Yes, he does. So what about…?
S1: Some socks.
L: Yes, maybe. Or perhaps something else? Let's see.
Does he collect stamps? – No, he doesn't. Does he take photos? Yes, he does. So what can we get him?
S2: A photo album.
S3: Or a book about photography.
usw.
Auf diese Weise werden Geschenkvorschläge für Ralph gemacht.

210

III Reproduzieren

Zuordnen

L: Now we want to find a present for Angela. I want someone to come out here, please. (S1), this is for you. It will help you to answer our questions about Angela. (S1 bekommt einen Zettel, auf dem Angelas Interessen in einer Tabelle aufgeführt sind. Diese Minitabelle wird auch an die Tafel bzw. auf den Tageslichtprojektor geschrieben. Während die Tabelle von S1 schon angekreuzt ist, wird es die an der Tafel erst im Laufe des folgenden Gesprächs.)

	play tennis	collect stamps	take photos	like pop music	classic-al music	paint	write letters
Angela	✔		✔		✔	✔	

L: (Richten Sie die erste Frage an S1): Now what about Angela? Does she play tennis? Say, »Yes, she does« or »No, she doesn't«.

S1: Yes, she does.

L: So let's put a tick (✔) here (deuten Sie auf die entsprechende Spalte). You draw a tick on your sheets, too. (Der Lehrer macht die entsprechende Eintragung in der Tabelle an der Tafel, und die Schüler nehmen sie in ihren Arbeitsblättern vor.)

L: Does she…? (Deuten Sie auf die Spalte *collect stamps.*)

S2: Does she collect stamps?

S1: No, she doesn't. (Die entsprechende Eintragung wird gemacht.)
  usw.

Geben Sie das jeweilige Muster vor. *(Does she … ?)*

Auf diese Weise werden Angelas Interessen festgestellt und in die Tabelle eingetragen. Anschließend werden Geschenkvorschläge gemacht.

L: So what can we get Angela for her birthday?

S1: Some tennis balls.

S2: A photo album.
  usw.

IV Produzieren

Zuordnen

Zunächst werden Martins und Dianes Interessen von den Schüler nach eigenem Gutdünken durch Haken gekennzeichnet.

    L: Put a tick in the boxes for Martin and Diane. Put the ticks where you like – under »play tennis«, under »collect stamps«, or under »take photos« and so on.

In Partnerarbeit versuchen die Schüler herauszufinden, wie ihre Partner die Haken verteilt haben. Gemeinsam werden dann Geschenkvorschläge gemacht.

    L: Now you need a partner. One of you (the person sitting near the window/on the left of the desk…) is Martin's friend. The other partner asks, »Does he play tennis?«, »Does he collect stamps?« and so on.
Martin's friend answers, »Yes, he does« or »No, he doesn't«. Then write down some ideas for a birthday present.

Folgende Strukturen werden als Gesprächshilfe angeschrieben:

Does she/he…?	Yes, she/he does. No, she/he doesn't.

Nachdem Martins Interessen besprochen worden sind, werden die Rollen vertauscht. Der Fragende ist nun *»Diane's friend«* und beantwortet Fragen über Dianes Interessen.

V Bewußtmachung

To find out what people do <u>regularly,</u> like hobbies, or what they are <u>interested in</u> we use the <u>simple present.</u>

do/does	+	infinitive	
Do	you	**like**	pop music?
Does	Ralph	**play**	tennis?

Simple present with future meaning:
question words + to do: when does the bus leave?

Legen Sie folgende Folie auf den Tageslichtprojektor oder benutzen Sie die Tafel.

Buses leaving for:		Arriving	Platform	Single	Return
Sheffield:	8.45–16.40	10.10–18.05	3	£ 4.75	£ 7.25
Reading: (change at Birmingham)	8.30–12.05 Sundays: only 12.05	15.40–19.15	1	£ 19	£ 35
Newmarket: (change at Cambridge)	8.45–12.20 Sundays: only 12.20	15.45–19.20	2	£ 25.50	£ 46.80

Buses arriving from:		Platform
Sheffield:	11.55–16.00	4
Reading:	12.10–15.48	1
Newmarket:	15.25	3

INFORMATION

I Demonstration

Schildern Sie die Situation auf der Folie. Schreiben Sie dabei einige der Fragen sowie unbekannten Wortschatz auf.

L: Colin works at Manchester bus station, at the information desk. He has to answer thousands of questions every day – questions like:

Where do I catch the bus to Sheffield?
How long does it take?
Where does the bus to Reading leave from?
Where do I change?
Where do buses from Newmarket arrive?
What time does the next one arrive?

When does the bus to Reading leave on Sundays?
How much does a single ticket cost?
How much does the return fare cost?

II Verstehen und Reagieren

Information erfragen und erteilen
Stellen Sie die Fragen zum abgebildeten Fahrplan, die von den Lernenden beantwortet werden.

L: Now let's see if you can help me. Look at the time-table. Tell me, please, where do I catch the bus to Newmarket?
S1: On platform 2.
L: How long does it take?
S2: Seven hours.
L: When does the next bus from Sheffield arrive?
S3: At eleven fifty-five.
usw.

Mögliche Fragen:
Where do I catch the bus to...?
Where do buses to/from ...leave from/arrive?
How long does it take (from... to...)?
What time does the next bus to... leave?
What time does the next bus from... arrive?
When does the bus to .../do buses to... leave on Sundays?
Where do I change?
How much does a single/return ticket/the ... fare cost?

III Reproduzieren

Information erfragen und erteilen
Abwechselnd spielen die Lernenden die Rolle des Auskunftgebenden. Benutzen Sie folgende Strukturen, um Fragen zum Fahrplan zu stellen. Geben Sie dabei das jeweilige Sprachmuster vor. Die Schüler gebrauchen dann die gleiche Struktur, um weitere Fragen zu stellen.
Es ist hilfreich, die Fragemöglichkeiten als *sentence switchboard* anzuschreiben.

Where	**do**	I catch the bus to…? I change? buses to … leave from? buses from … arrive?
What time When	**does**	it leave? the next bus to/from… leave/arrive? the bus to … leave on Sundays?
	do	buses to … leave on Sundays?
How long	**does**	it take from… to…?
How much	**does**	the single/return fare cost?

L: Who wants to come out here and be Colin?
Now (S1 – als Colin), let's see if you can help me.
Good morning. Where do I catch the bus to Sheffield, please?

S1: On platform 3.

L: Thank you. Goodbye.
Now I want someone else to come to Colin's desk and ask another question.

S2: Good morning. Where do I catch the bus to Newmarket, please?
(Als Sprechimpuls zeigen Sie auf die Struktur.)

S1: …

Mehrere Schüler stellen mit Hilfe der gleichen Struktur weitere Fragen, z.B. *Where do* I change/buses to… leave from/buses from… arrive? Nachdem einige Schüler zu Wort gekommen sind, werden in der gleichen Weise die weiteren Strukturen geübt.

L: What time does the next bus to… leave?

S1: (als Colin) At…

S2: Good morning. What time does the next bus from… arrive?
usw.

IV Produzieren

Information erfragen und erteilen
Die Szene wird ohne Hilfe des Lehrers gespielt und ohne daß die Strukturen vorgegeben werden.

L: Now I want two people to come out here.
(S1), you're Colin and you, (S2), want some information.

S1: Good morning. (Can I help you?)

S2: Good morning. Where/When/How much…?
usw.

V Bewußtmachung

When we ask questions about things that are regular and fixed and we use a question word like <u>what, where, when, how?</u> we need the verb »to do«.

question word	to do	
When		the bus to London leave?
Where	**does**	the Sheffield bus arrive?
Where	**do**	I catch it?
How long		...?
...		

Die Lernenden können weitere Beispiele aus der vorausgegangenen Lektion suchen.

Some, somebody, something

I Demonstration

Führen Sie die Wörter *some, somebody* und *something* ein, indem Sie verschiedene Bitten und Anforderungen an die Klasse richten, z.B.:

L: Can somebody lend me a biro/open the window/clean the board/... please?

I need some paper/pencils/felt-tips/... please.

Can somebody give me something to write with?

Tell me something about yourself/your family, pets, hobbies/... (Geben Sie den Lernenden Gelegenheit, kurz darauf zu antworten.)

Sprechen Sie nun über die Folie. Nur die ersten sechs Bilder sind zu sehen, die restlichen sind abgedeckt.

L: We often have to ask people for things, don't we? Look at Don. He's asking his father for something. He says, »Can I have some money, please?«

But he doesn't only ask for things. He gives things to people, too. Look at the second picture. Here he says, »I've got some flowers for you, Mum.«
(Bild 3) In this picture he says, »Listen. There's somebody at the door.«
(Bild 4) In this one his mother says, »Can somebody shut the window, please?«
(Bild 5) Here Don wants something again. He says, »Can I have something to eat?«
(Bild 6) This is a picture of Don's sister. She's on holiday in Scotland. Don writes to her and says, »Tell me something about Scotland.«

II Verstehen und Reagieren

Hörverstehen: Zuordnen
Decken Sie die restlichen Bilder auf und lesen Sie die Sätze vor (s. unten). Die Lernenden versuchen herauszufinden, wer welchen Satz gesprochen hat.

L: Now look at these pictures. Listen, who do you think said this: »Can you lend me <u>some</u> felt-tips?«

S1: Brian.

L: And who said this, »I met <u>somebody</u> from Australia last week«?

S2: Margaret.

usw.

Weitere Sätze mit Lösungen:

»Can I have <u>something</u> to drink, please?« – Penny

»I've got <u>some</u> new records.« – Carol

»Can <u>somebody</u> help me with my homework?« – Roger

»I've got <u>something</u> for you.« – Alice

»Would you like <u>some</u> coffee?« – Mrs Davies

»Can <u>somebody</u> open the door for me, please?« – Mr Davies

»Have you got <u>something</u> to read on the train?« – Harry

»I need <u>some</u> new socks.« – Marilyn

»I saw <u>somebody</u> in your garden last night.« – Mrs Kent

»There's <u>something</u> on your coat.« – Sally

III Reproduzieren

Bitten und Angebote

Fertigen Sie Satzkarten an, die in folgende Strukturgruppen aufgeteilt sind:

A. Can you lend me **some** …, please?
    Can I have **some** …, please?
    I've got **some**…
    I need **some**…

B. Can I have **something** to (eat/ …), please?
    Can you lend me **something** to (write with/ …), please?
    I've got **something** for you.
    Tell me **something** about…

C. Can **somebody** lend me…, please?
    Can **somebody** (open…), please?

Auf jeder Karte sind für die Satzlücken verschiedene Auswahlmöglichkeiten angegeben, z.B. felt-tips, orange juice. Da sich einige dieser Gegenstände nicht im Klassenzimmer befinden, sollten Sie diese entweder mitbringen oder Sie fertigen Bildkarten an. Der Wortschatz kann der jeweiligen Klasse angepaßt werden. Einige Vorschläge: 3–4 *comics*, 3–4 *books*, 3–4 *records* (oder entsprechende Bildkarten mit jeweils 3–4 der betreffenden Gegenstände); *English money, food and drink (chocolate, orange juice, cake, apples, tea).*

Satzkarten
Wenn nicht anders vermerkt, stellen Sie für jede Struktur eine Satzkarte her.

A. (Name), can you lend me some …, please?
    (felt-tips, money, paper, comics)

A. (Name), can I have some …, please?
    (felt-tips, paper, comics, chocolate)

A. (Name), I've got some… Would you like some?
    (3–4 Karten mit jeweils Abbildungen von 2–3 *comics,* 2–3 *sweets, orange juice,* oder *a bar of chocolate)*

A. I need some…
    (felt-tips, paper)

B. (Name), can I have something to …, please?
    (write with, write on, eat, drink, read)

B. (Name), can you lend me something to …, please?
    (write with, write on, read)

B. (Name), I've got something for you.
    (3–4 Karten mit jeweils Abbildungen von 2–3 *comics,* 2–3 *sweets, bunch of flowers,* oder *a bar of chocolate)*

B. (Name), tell me something about…
    (your family, your hobbies)

C. Can somebody lend me …, please?
    (a biro, a ruler, some felt-tips, some paper)

C. Can somebody …, please?
    (shut, open the window; shut, open the door)

Schreiben Sie folgende mögliche Antworten auf:
– Here you are.
– Thanks.
– Sorry, I need it/them myself.

- Yes, please.
- No thanks. I've got some, too.

Teilen Sie die Karten der Gruppe A an einige Schüler aus und heften Sie die Bildkarten an die Tafel. Geben Sie das Dialogmuster vor.

L: (S1), can you lend me some felt-tips, please?
   (Deuten Sie auf die Antwortmöglichkeiten.)
S1: Here you are. (Leiht Ihnen die eigenen.)
L: Who's got a card? Now you start.
S2: (S3), I've got some sweets. (Zeigt seine illustrierte Bildkarte.) Would you like some?
S3: Yes, please.
S2: (Gibt S3 die Satzkarte.) Here you are.
S3: Thanks.
   usw.

Nachdem diese Struktur genügend geübt wurde, sammeln Sie die Satzkarten ein und teilen die der Gruppe B aus. Geben Sie wieder das Dialogmuster vor.

L: (S1), can I have something to drink, please?
S1: (Holt die entsprechende an die Tafel angeheftete Bildkarte.) Here you are.
L: Thanks. Who can go on?
S2: (S3), I've got something for you. (Gibt S3 seine illustrierte Satzkarte.)
S3: Thanks.
   usw.

Nach einiger Zeit werden die Satzkarten eingesammelt und die der Gruppe C ausgeteilt.

L: Can somebody open the door, please?
S1: (Öffnet die Tür.)
L: Thanks. Who can go on?
   usw.

IV Produzieren

Bitten und Angebote
Die Aktivität wird nun ohne Ihre Hilfe fortgesetzt. Teilen Sie dazu alle Satzkarten aus. Die Strukturen werden nicht mehr gruppenweise geübt, sondern durcheinander.

L: Who wants to start?
S1: (S2), can I have something to eat, please?
S2: (Sucht eine entsprechende Bildkarte aus und überreicht sie S1.) Here you are.
S1: Thanks.

L: Who can go on?
S3: (S4), tell me something about your family.
S4: I've got two sisters. One is ten…
     usw.

V Bewußtmachung

We use **some, something** and **somebody**
a) when we <u>want</u> something and <u>think</u> we can get it:
     I need <u>some</u> felt-tips.
     Can I have <u>something</u> to eat, please?
     Can <u>somebody</u> lend me a ruler?

b) when we <u>offer</u> things to people:
     Would you like <u>some</u> chocolate?
     I've got <u>something</u> for you.

Sie können auch auf die folgenden häufigen Fehler hinweisen *another one* anstatt *somebody else;* *another thing* anstatt *something else.*

Bibliographie

Asher, James J.: *Learning another language through actions: The complete teacher's guide book.* Los Gatos/CA: Sky Oaks Productions 1977

Billows, F.L.: *The Techniques of Language Teaching.* London: Longman 1961

Brown, Roger: »Introduction« in: Snow, C.E./Ferguson, C.A.: *Talking to Children.* Cambridge: University Press 1977

Bruner, J.S.: *Child's talk.* New York: Norton 1983

Butzkamm, Wolfgang: *Psycholinguistik des Fremdsprachenunterrichts.* Tübingen: R. Franke 1989

Chomsky, Noam: »A Review of B.F. Skinner's ›Verbal Behaviour‹«, *Language* 35 (Heft 1), S. 26–58, 1958

Chomsky, Noam: *Reflections on Language.* New York: Pantheon 1975

Chomsky, Noam: *Lectures on government and binding.* Dordrecht: Foris 1981

Chomsky, Noam: *Knowledge of language.* New York: Praeger 1986

Clashen, Harald: *Spracherwerb in der Kindheit.* Tübingen: Narr 1982

Crystal, David: *Listen to your child. A parent's guide to children's language.* Harmondsworth: Penguin 1986

Dulay, Heidi/Burt, Marina/Krashen, Stephan: *Language two.* New York, Oxford: OUP 1982

Felix, S.: *Cognition and language growth.* Dordrecht: Foris 1987

Göller, H.: »Lernpsychologische und kognitive Grammatikarbeit im Französischunterricht«, *Praxis des neusprachlichen Unterrichts,* 4/1982, S. 401–408

Hinz, Klaus: *Grammatik im Unterricht.* Moderner Englischunterricht: Arbeitshilfen für die Praxis 8. Hannover: Schroedel; Dortmund: Lensing 1977

Holt, John: *How Children Learn.* Harmondsworth: Penguin 1970

Hüllen, Werner: *Linguistik und Englischunterricht.* Heidelberg: Quelle & Meyer 1971

Krashen, Stephan: *Second Language Acquisition and Second Language Learning.* Oxford: Pergamon Press 1981 und *Principles and Practice in Second Language Acquisition.* Oxford: Pergamon Press 1982

Macnamara, J.: »The cognitive basis of language learning in infants«, *Psychological Review* 79, S. 1–13

Mindt, Dieter: »Probleme des pragmalinguistischen Ansatzes in der Fremdsprachendidaktik«, *Die Neueren Sprachen,* Heft 3/4, S. 340–356

Moerk, E.L.: »Analytik, synthetic, abstracting and word-class-defining aspects of verbal mother–child interactions«, *Journal of Psycholinguistic Research,* Heft 14/3, 1985, S. 265

Palmer, H.E./Palmer, D.: *English through actions.* London: Longman 1925/1958

Piepho, H.E.: *Kommunikative Kompetenz als übergeordnetes Lernziel im Englischunterricht.* Dornburg-Frickhofen: Frankonius 1974

Rizzi, L.: *Issues in Italian syntax.* Dordrecht: Foris 1982

Skinner, B.F.: *Verbal Behaviour.* New York: Meredith 1957

Stern, Clara/Stern, William: *Monographien über die seelische Entwicklung des Kindes.* Leipzig: Barth 1928

Wode, Henning: »Die Entwicklung des sprachlichen Hörens und seine Bedeutung für einen zeitgemäßen Deutschunterricht«, *Der Deutschunterricht,* 5/90, S. 19–24, bes. S. 30 ff.

Hans Lobentanzer
Jeder sein eigener Englischlehrer
Fehlerfrei in Grammatik und Wortschatz
Übungen und Lösungen
Ca. 100 Seiten, geb. ca. DM 20.– Best.-Nr. 03228-1

Reden, Schreiben und Lesen vollzieht sich in Sinnzusammenhängen; dies sind meist
Sätze. In diesen lassen sich Grammatik und gängiger Wortschatz einschleifen.
Der Autor hat fast 2000 deutsche Sätze zusammengestellt. Er geht vom Leichten zum
Schweren vor, zeigt in Hinweisen und kurzgefaßten Regeln, wie die Grammatik-Hürden
zu nehmen sind und erweitert in 12 Kapiteln den Wortschatz nochmals beträchtlich. Im
unteren Teil jeder Seite sind alle Sätze im Kleindruck ins Englische übersetzt.
Für alle, die ihr Englisch auffrischen und/oder verbessern wollen. Vor allem für Lehrer
und Kursteilnehmer in der Erwachsenenbildung.

Gertrud Walter
Kompendium Didaktik Englisch
140 Seiten, Pbck. DM 22,– Best.-Nr. 02308-8

Der Band wendet sich an Studierende für ein Lehramt sowie an Lehrer der verschiedenen Schultypen und Schulstufen. Er gibt eine Einführung in die fachdi-
daktische Diskussion sowie in die Probleme des Englischunterrichts und vermittelt
Anregungen für die Unterrichtspraxis.

Paul Kremer / Detlef Nimtz
Deutsche Grammatik
Umfassende Arbeitsanleitungen. Mit Übungen und Lösungen.
8., völlig neu bearb. Auflage. Ca. 180 Seiten, Pbck. ca. DM 28,–
Best.-Nr. 03163-3

Die Kenntnis dieser sehr gut aufgebauten, klar verständlich und übersichtlich ge-
schriebenen Grammatik, die alle Teile der deutschen Sprache behandelt, fördert sowohl
die Fähigkeit des Hörens und Lesens als auch die des Sprechens und Schreibens. Sie
ist als Grundlage des Deutschunterrichts, aber auch zum Selbststudium geeignet.

Preisänderungen vorbehalten

Ehrenwirth Verlag München